The Forgotten People: Updated

THE FORGOTTEN PEOPLE: UPDATED

Edited by Paul Ritchie

Jeparit Press

Published by Connor Court Publishing under the imprint: Jeparit Press 2018

Copyright © Nick Cater 2018

ALL RIGHTS RESERVED. This book contains material protected under International and Federal Copyright Laws and Treaties. Any unauthorised reprint or use of this material is prohibited. No part of this book may be reproduced or transmitted in any form or by any means, electronic or mechanical, including photocopying, recording, or by any information storage and retrieval system without express written permission from the publisher.

Connor Court Publishing Pty Ltd, PO Box 7257
Redland Bay QLD 4165
sales@connorcourt.com
www.connorcourtpublishing.com.au

ISBN: 9781925826012

Cover design by Shireen Liversedge

Series Editor: Nick Cater

Cover Design: Shireen Liversedge

Jeparit Press is an imprint of Connor Court Publishing in conjunction with the Menzies Research Centre.

Menzies Research Centre
R.G. Menzies House
1 Macquarie St
Barton
ACT 2600
www.menziesrc.org

Printed in Australia.

"A party needs to know what it stands for, in order to stay faithful to the people it elected, and it needs to communicate what it stands for until the bell rings"

– the Rt Hon R G Menzies, Albury 1944

* * * * *

For Heather Henderson – who has supported and stood by her father's party since the day it was founded.

Contents

Foreword x
Malcolm Turnbull

Preface xvi
Paul Ritchie

1. The Forgotten People 1
Paul Ritchie

2. Freedom of Speech and Expression 15
James Paterson

3. Freedom of Worship 23
Julian Leeser

4. Freedom from Want 33
Ken Wyatt

5. Freedom from Fear 41
Nick Cater

6. Empire Control of an Empire War 47
Tony Abbott

7. What the British are doing in this War 53
Georgina Downer

8. Hatred as an Instrument of War Policy 61
Concetta Fierravanti-Wells

9. Scrap Iron for Japan 67
Andrew Bragg

10. The Censorship 77
Peter Phelps

11. The New Minister to Washington 83
Josh Frydenberg

12. Our American Allies 89
    Andrew Shearer
13. Lend Lease 95
    Linda Reynolds
14. Women in War 101
    Peta Credlin
15. Paying for the War 109
    Chris Rath
16. Post War Planning 115
    Paul Fletcher
17. Rationalisation of Industry 125
    Jane Hume
18. Taxing the Shareholder 131
    Kelly O'Dwyer
19. Has Capitalism Failed? 137
    Adam Boyton
20. The Drink Problem 143
    Alan Tudge
21. Is Inflation a Bogey? 149
    Louise Ahern
22. Compulsory Unionism 153
    Michaelia Cash
23. The Function of an Opposition in Parliament 159
    Christopher Pyne
24. The Opposition's Duty 163
    Scott Ryan
25. The Government and Ourselves 169
    Tony Smith
26. Sea Power 173
    Cam Hawker

27. The Statute of Westminster 179
   Dean Smith
28. Schools and the War 185
   Ross Fox
29. The Moral Element in Total War 191
   Jim Molan
30. The Law and the Citizen 199
   Natalie Ward
31. The Nature of Democracy 207
   Nicolle Flint
32. The Sickness of Democracy 211
   Trent Zimmerman
33. The Achievement of Democracy 219
   Jonathon Duniam
34. The Task of Democracy 225
   Peta Seaton
35. The Importance of Cheerfulness 231
   Tim Wilson

The Contributors 237

FOREWORD

Malcolm Turnbull

Just over seventy-five years have passed since Bob Menzies commenced his radio talks that were subsequently published as *The Forgotten People*.

When Menzies commenced his broadcasts in 1942, it was during a time that Churchill described as the 'hinge of fate'. The world was at war and it was as though one catastrophe was being piled onto another. Pearl Harbour had been bombed, the pride of the American Navy had been sunk or disabled, save its aircraft carriers mercifully. Singapore had fallen. 22,000 Australian soldiers were prisoners of the Japanese. Those that weren't, were in the most part in the Middle East.

The Japanese seemed as irrepressible and just two weeks before Menzies gave his Forgotten People broadcast, there was the Battle of the Coral Sea. For the first time, the hinge of fate started to turn. Australians and Americans from the United States Navy and the Royal Australian Navy, serving together under a joint command, succeeded in turning back the Japanese.

Following these successes, Australians could begin coolly to consider, in the absence of bravado, that the tide had turned. In was in this setting that Menzies through his radio broadcasts set out his eloquent and principled vision for Australia beyond the war.

Liberal democracies in those years seemed caught between the hammer of fascism and the anvil of communism, each offering the vision of the mighty all-knowing State.

So in his 37 broadcasts, Menzies spoke up for the foot soldiers

Foreword

in Edmund Burke's small platoons, equally forgotten in the boardrooms of the mighty corporations and in the back rooms of the Trades Hall.

With a common sense that resonates right up to today, he dismissed those who try to wage a hate-filled class war and divide Australians and turn them on each other. He steered resolutely to the centre ground and put his faith in the goodwill, the common sense and the enterprise of his fellow Australians.

Menzies believed, as we his successors believe today, that the task of government is not as others would say, to tell Australians what is best but rather to enable them to do their best.

He yearned to increase their opportunities; expand their horizons, so that they could pursue their dreams for themselves and for their children.

Menzies had not long lost the Prime Ministership when he took to making his weekly broadcasts. Politically this was his wilderness period, but there is no rancour or bitterness in his broadcasts. He is as calm as he is considered, as elegant as he is erudite.

His humour shines through. In one broadcast, asked whether so much war and destruction showed Christianity has failed, he suggests we should try practising it first.

He resisted populism when state premiers were condemned for challenging in the courts the federal takeover of income tax, he defended their constitutional right to do so and spoke up for the rule of law.

Security under the law, in Erskine's phrase he said: "is not something precariously dependent upon the whim of a mob. It is that security to which a man may confidently and calmly appeal, even though every other's hand may be against him. The law's greatest benefits are for the minority man; the individual".

And when he introduced as Prime Minister in the previous

year, the national security bill that gave sweeping powers to the Government to control the economy, he did so with this sober warning; "The greatest tragedy that could overcome a country, would be for it to fight a successful war in defence of liberty and lose its own liberty in the process."

In many broadcasts Menzies spoke not of the war efforts or future policies; instead, he spoke of our character as a country. He rejected the idea that everything was political, rather he chose to speak about who we are and what we value.

In April 1942 – before the Battle of the Coral Sea – Menzies spoke about hatred. During a time when Australians were becoming increasingly aware of the wickedness of their then Pacific enemy, he decried a government campaign that he felt was designed to encourage Australians to hate the Japanese. This is what he said;

"It is an offence to an honest citizen to imagine that the cold, evil and repulsive spirit of racial hatred must be substituted for honest and brave indignation, if his greatest effort is to be obtained."

"Peace may be all sorts of things – a real end of war, a mere exhaustion, an armed interlude before the next struggle. But it will only be by a profound stirring in the hearts of men that we shall reach goodwill."

"In short, when this war is over, we all hope to live in a better world in which both Germans and Japanese – violently purged of their lust for material power – will be able to live and move in amity with ourselves."

It says much about the character of the man that he could write such generous words in such hard days.

This book, however, is not just about reminding us about what Liberals believe. It is also about reflecting on our shared Liberal values in our times. It is to look forward.

The Forgotten People: Updated reflects the breadth of thinking of the heirs of Menzies. In 1944, Menzies created a party out of 18 different political organisations and he fused an innate conservatism with a modern liberalism.

To use the analogy of the Member for Goldstein which eloquently captures how these strands powerfully reinforce each other even today: our Party's conservatism is an anchor that points to our values, tempers our exuberances and reminds us of our history and traditions; and our Party's liberalism is our compass that points to freedom, opportunity, and a future where more Australians can share in our country's bounty.

Our second longest serving Prime Minister, John Howard once called the Liberal Party a "broad church". He is right. Menzies believed that the Liberal Party must reflect the breadth of our country and not be owned by any self-serving group. We continue to be that today: we are owned by no union, foreign interest, or business association. We are truly a grassroots party, accountable to our tens of thousands of members who are a microcosm of the nation that we serve.

Together, we share the hope of Menzies that "our objective must be to build a balanced, strong, progressive and civilised nation in which advances are shared by all sections of the people." This book reflects that hope.

In taking the same chapter titles as Menzies used three quarters of a century ago, it does not cover every topic that we might expect today.

The topic list for a series of radio broadcasts by an Australian politician today would look very different, if indeed he or she chose to speak on radio. Today, a politician might opt for Facebook or YouTube to speak directly to the people.

Nor does this book claim or seek to be a rigid reflection of my views or that of the Government. Instead it reflects Menzies' hope that his Party would be a community of thinkers, each striving to interpret the times as best as he or she sees fit. Such a party encourages debate, contends for ideas and asks regularly, what can we learn from the past as we prepare to face the future?

As Senator Scott Ryan points out in his chapter, debate should not be confused with division. Debate is, in fact, the pre-requisite and foundation for unity and the expression of our shared values.

When I became Prime Minister I said: "There has never been a more exciting time to be alive than today and there has never been a more exciting time to be an Australian." This book reflects that same optimism. Of course, there are challenges, there always have been and always will be, but our values and vision give us the strength and fortitude to take them on.

You will see from the writings of my colleagues that the Liberal and National Government is true to its liberal values and the beliefs and hopes of Menzies.

We believe in free trade, because trade is the foundation for a bigger Australia; we believe in lower taxes because lower taxes drive investment and jobs, we believe in choice in schools because all Australians should be free to live their values; we believe in personal responsibility because from it flows the strength to face our daily challenges; we believe in strong borders because our immigration system must serve Australia's national interest and we continue to hold fast to our alliances because the world is best served by free markets and free nations.

Our economy is growing, more than one million new jobs have been created since 2013, and we are keeping Australia strong through major investments in security and defence, infrastructure, health and education. We are doing all of this while living within our means, and continuing to repair the budget.

It is to the credit of the editor Paul Ritchie that he has brought

Foreword

together such an array of liberals across Australia for this project honouring our founder. The Menzies Research Centre, under the leadership of Nick Cater, continues its tremendous work advancing the cause of Liberalism to a new generation of Australians.

This 2018 edition of *The Forgotten People* is a worthy contribution to the Liberal Party's great quest of advancing the cause of Australia. I commend it to you.

May 2018

PREFACE

Paul Ritchie

Before there was a Liberal Party, there was *The Forgotten People*.

The Forgotten People, first published 75 years ago, is the sacred text of the Liberal Party. The text was taken from 37 separate radio broadcasts given by Robert Menzies during 1942.

At that time Menzies was a freshly minted former prime minister having served in the office from 1939 to 1941. In 1942, he was considered 'washed-up' at the age of 47.

Politically, Menzies first stint as prime minister was not glorious. But governing is more than politics and history is kinder about the work he did addressing Australia's under-preparedness for war in the Pacific.

He had become prime minister in 1939, following the death of Joe Lyons, and just months before the start of the Second World War.

Menzies was the most gifted man on his side of politics but he had never tasted defeat. He had won scholarship after scholarship; prevailed in cases before the High Court; had been Victorian state Attorney-General and Deputy Premier in his 30s; a federal MP by 40; and Prime Minister at 45. He was confident, arrogant, and carried himself with more than a touch of superiority. Maybe that was why he only won the leadership by just 4 votes against the 77-year-old Billy Hughes.

When Menzies first visited the Governor-General to be commissioned he was asked "Mr Menzies, how long do you think your government will last?"

"About six weeks Your Excellency", he replied.

"Well, that will do for a start", said the Governor-General.

It would last 28 months.

Menzies began his prime ministership with a deeply divided party, a deeply divided government, and a deeply divided country on the eve of war.

The government had to prepare for war even though the country was ambivalent about it. They were ambivalent because of their experiences in the Great War.

The Great War they were told was to be the 'war to end all wars'. It was to be quick, glorious and reflect the greatness of Empire. It was anything but.

Even today, the statistics are staggering. From an Australian population of just under five million, 417,000 enlisted; 332,000 served overseas; 152,000 were wounded; and 61,000 never came home. Of the 270,000 who returned, more than half returned wounded. The suffering continued after the war, with tens of thousands of families dealing with alcohol, addictions, violence and mental illness, as men struggled with undiagnosed post-traumatic stress. Little wonder both sides of politics felt reluctance about another conflict.

Sir Percy Spender wrote after the end of the Second World War "even after Dunkirk, there was in Australia no unity of opinion, no sense of need for national sacrifice such as existed in Britain."

While the settings and framework for victory was set in those first years under Menzies, frankly, we weren't winning in 1940 and 1941. The government felt every blow of those early years – particularly as Menzies desperately tried to engage Britain in providing more resources for the defence of Singapore.

It was relentless in the media as well. Paul Hasluck wrote there was "something rather indecent about the glee which Australian writers and speakers seemed to display whenever they found that something was going wrong, and the lesser concern with either what had been done or remained to do".

Later in life, Menzies would say of his first stint as Prime Minister that he was "aloof from my own supporters" and had "yet to acquire the common touch".

In a time of national peril, Menzies chose to ignore the politics of the time and immerse himself in the job of wartime defence and he paid a heavy political price for that.

During mid-1941, the walls were closing in on him. His colleagues whispered about his leadership, his opponents stood waiting for its end and the united purpose that Australia needed was suffering as a result.

In August that year, Menzies resigned as prime minister. He jumped before anyone pushed. As the Liberal Party's historian, David Kemp puts it "Menzies' resignation was the act of a man sickened by political manoeuvring and division on his side at a time of supreme national peril".

Within six weeks, the minority government that he was part of fell and Menzies contemplated political life from Opposition. It was in the wilderness, with his lifetime upward trajectory destroyed, that Menzies contemplated the future.

His brother Frank suggested that if he was to rebuild his shattered political career he needed to reflect on what was his underlying philosophy. So in 1942, Menzies started a series of weekly radio broadcasts that in time would be bound into a book and become known as *The Forgotten People*.

Like any entertaining broadcaster, Menzies mixed and matched his subjects – some broadcasts were deeply philosophical, others whimsical and conversational, and others simply reflected the passing issues of the day.

Throughout the broadcasts there was discipline, focus and clarity in Menzies' words. He was a former prime minister of a country at war that was facing great peril. He could not play politics. When he chose to speak of areas of political contention, he did so with respect and with a laser focus on the values and ideas at stake. In no place does he question the integrity or patriotism of his opponents. These choices were a reflection of both his character and his political judgment and resulted in the broadcasts focusing on timeless values.

What he did in the broadcasts was lay out a clear political philosophy: mutual respect, because the nation is but the sum of our human relationships; personal responsibility "because the best things are done by man, not men"; civic mindedness because "intelligent citizenry" is the best defence against tyranny; parliamentary government because only it can deliver the rule of law; and the advancement of Australia based on reward for effort.

Australians, he believed, must embrace freedom in all its forms because "the real freedoms are to worship, to think, to speak, to choose, to be ambitious, to be independent, to be industrious, to acquire skill, to seek reward. These are the real freedoms, for these are of the essence of the nature of man."

Yet this required a different Australian culture than the one that permeated the 1930s and the early 1940s.

Menzies belief was that despite engaging in a war against fascism and militarism that was requiring great sacrifice, the character of the nation was weak instead of strong.

During the 1920s and 1930s, Australians had increasingly turned on each other rather than to each other. Class wars, sectarian hatreds and a distrust of others had taken their toll as Australians focused on what they could get from the nation rather than what they could contribute to it.

Menzies nailed the challenge with these words:

> To discourage ambition, to envy success, to hate achieved superiority, to distrust independent thought, to sneer at and impute false motive for public service – these are the maladies of modern democracy in particular. Yet ambition, effort, thinking and readiness to serve are not only the design and objectives of self-government, but are the essential conditions of its success.

The essence of *The Forgotten People* is the belief that Australia future prosperity was to be found in giving the middle class more choice, more freedom and more reward.

Menzies' world of freedom and choice did not mean he wanted a Hobbesian dog-eat-dog world. Far from it, he despised class war and "the disease of thinking that the community is divided into the rich and relatively idle, and the laborious poor, and that every social and political controversy can be resolved into the question: whose side are you on?"

He hated 'base politics' that seek to incite anger at other Australians with the goal of political gain, not realising that it silently weakens the bonds between us all. To him, it was as bad as its political cousin 'pragmatic politics' which governs by the compromise of vested interest rather than being guided by national interest.

To Menzies, the foundation of Australian life was always found in "homes material, homes human and homes spiritual". He grasped that politics was more than a fistful of dollars, or the advancement of one group over another. It has a deeper purpose, which is to create the right settings for Australians to lead happy and meaningful lives.

In his eyes, the advancement of Australia needed a shift in thinking. What was needed was not more dependence on government, though government should provide solace to "those whose fate has compelled to live on the bounty of the state"; rather Australia needed a "fierce independence of spirit" that would propel the nation.

However, that fiercely independent spirit must first be nurtured and encouraged. This meant changing the mindset from taking to giving.

As he said "the great vice of democracy – a vice which is extracting a bitter retribution at this moment – is that for a generation we have been busy getting ourselves on the list of beneficiaries and removing ourselves from the list of contributors, as if somewhere there was somebody's wealth and somebody else's effort on which we could thrive".

It was from these rich philosophical timbers that a great institution was built – the Liberal Party of Australia.

In 1944 Menzies set out to create a political party which in his words "would alter the course of Australian history" – and surely his party – our party – has fulfilled that promise.

As we know, Menzies went on to become our longest serving prime minister and to have a profoundly different leadership what was envisaged in the early 1940s. In total, he was elected eight times as prime minister. His record might never be eclipsed. To appropriate a sporting acronym that is popular these days: 'he's the GOAT'. The Greatest Of All Time.

In reflecting on the 75th anniversary of the publication of *The Forgotten People*, the political heirs of Menzies are taking up his challenge (first expressed by Tennyson): "To strive, to seek, to find, and not to yield".

Thirty-five of the political heirs of Menzies are interpreting him for our age. This reflection from Liberals old and young; indigenous and immigrant; regional and city dweller; from within our Parliaments and outside them; and from every state in the Commonwealth, take the original chapter topics of *The Forgotten People* and apply them to today.

We have engaged in this project with the blessing of Sir Robert's daughter Heather Henderson and the Menzies Research Centre which has responsibility for guarding and fostering his legacy.

Naturally, some chapter titles might appear to be no longer relevant, after all, we are not in the midst of fighting a world war. Still, even in the original text, there is found underlying ideals and values.

The authors have all captured the ethos of Menzies that politics is both "a science and an art". The science of politics is policy and the art of politics is its implementation. Politics then and now must reflect both.

True, there will always be the game of politics, and with it the daily commentary of who is up and who is down, as well as the observations of who has made progress and who has erred. But the game of politics, must never triumph over the purpose of politics. The science and art must be drawn together to build a better, stronger, and fairer country.

Of course, we must win elections. But we must not lose the heroic. As Menzies said in an address to the Young Liberals in 1962

> We are not here just to win an election. Nor are you here just to help win an election. We are here to win something, to do something for our country. And therefore we must, at all times, try to behave according to the standards of statesmanship and not just according to the standards of vote-getting. I am the last person to deny that unless you have votes, you have singularly little opportunity for the statesmanship. But getting votes is not the be-all and end-all. We must have some picture in our minds of what we

want to do. This perhaps is more important even for the young than it is important for me. Though it is superbly important for me because I have the major responsibility in government. But it is vastly important for you.

These essays reflect the science and art of politics and the sure hope of unchanging Liberal values.

In replicating the very titles chosen by Menzies, we have chosen not to make this book a manifesto. Indeed, the original version was not a manifesto either. But in its entirety, it covers most of the challenges of modern public policy. It also reminds us that many of the debates of the last 75 years have not changed.

Forty years have passed since Australia's longest serving prime minister passed away. As a child, I watched his grand funeral on a black and white television in a fifth grade classroom, little appreciating his true impact on our country and indirectly, on my own life. In time, I came to realise he was the pivot that set Australia's course for the second half of the 20th century.

It is easy in this age of brutal tribalism, populism and short-termism to be disheartened. When we look to the future, pessimism runs rife. The tectonic plates seem to be shifting against liberal democracies and the values of enterprise, freedom and the individual. The advent of instant communications and commentary has also seen many of us lose sight of the values and history we share. Instead, our focus is on the daily fights and personalities that represent our political tribes.

Yet, it is in looking to the past that we can find courage and strength to face the challenges of our times. We see other generations heroically facing down the dangers of fascism and militarism; we see them sacrificing and living selflessly; and we see the strong chords of nationhood emerge from the camaraderie of its citizens. The 1940s were not easy times, but they were defining times when human civilization was protected and an unprecedented era of prosperity was born.

In creating a modern Liberal Party, Menzies sought to create a "community of thought" guided by values as well as the times. Menzies said that our principal objective as Liberals is to "build a balanced, strong, progressive, and civilised nation in which advances are shared by all sections of the people". I am confident that this edition of *The Forgotten People* written by this enduring community of thought will contribute mightily to that great goal.

1
THE FORGOTTEN PEOPLE

Paul Ritchie

They were called forgotten so that they would be remembered. The advancement of Australia has not been the result of force, might, or even luck, as some suggest, it has been the result of the sweat, thrift, virtue and enterprise of Australia's middle class.

To Australia, the middle class are the lifesaver's zinc, the firefighter's hose, the digger's slouch hat, and the shopkeeper's keys. There is no Australia without their sacrifice and efforts.

They pay their taxes – and the taxes of others as well; they turn up at school tuckshops when others are seemingly too busy; they pack hampers in churches; and raise kids, who in time, will become as good and as decent as the parents who fret over them.

Embodying family, community, love of country and others over self, they are the quiet ones so easily forgotten in a world that seeks attention and cries out for more and more. They demand no benefit, they only ask that their efforts and sacrifices not be penalised or mocked.

Through self-sacrifice, frugality and saving they put off until tomorrow the pleasure of life, because they understand that tomorrow's opportunities are always purchased through effort today.

The best people said Menzies, "are not those who leave it to the other fellow", but those who through thrift and self-sacrifice, establish homes and bring up families and add to the national pool of skills and savings, and who simply aspire to sit "under their own vine and fig-tree owing nothing to anyone".

In a world of short-cuts, they are surely tempted to take an easier path and become takers rather than givers, leaners rather than lifters, complainers rather than problem solvers.

Others might think they can ride freely on the efforts and income of the forgotten people, but these free-riders who rob others, eventually rob themselves of their own self-respect, purpose and capacity to strive.

While at times the forgotten people might look with envy at their freeloading brethren, it is their own efforts that make them a strong, self-sustaining and self-mobilising force capable of adapting to change. It is why they are foundational to the country we share.

The forgotten people are not just foundational to Australia, but to the political party that Menzies founded. Because Menzies' party embodies the forgotten people, it remains their best hope, and in turn, the nation's. They deserve "the full measure of security", because they are our security and the sure foundation of our country.

To the forgotten people, life is an invitation to accept responsibility and with this responsibility comes wisdom, strength, resilience, and confidence.

Three great forces conspire against the advancement of the forgotten people and in turn, Australia in this 21st century. They are the same forces they conspired against it during the last century: a lack of respect for the enterprise of others; the manipulation of false class conflicts that weaken the nation; and the triumph of the game of politics over the purpose of politics.

A nation of contributors

Australia was called a 'common-wealth' because our fortunes might rise, our fortunes might fall, but our strength and progress lies with each other.

No matter our race, gender, creed, sexuality, political or

economic background, we share the same land, same heritage, and same future. We are gifted by God to be the only nation with a continent to itself.

"What is the state but us?" asked Menzies three-quarters of a century ago. He understood that when we all seek to take, and to be a beneficiary rather than a benefactor, we take from ourselves. If the 'common-wealth' is just built on withdrawals than deposits, then poverty and its fruits await us all.

A nation of contributors advances us all. Those who claim we can all be beneficiaries defy belief. They speak of a world of dividends without effort, food without planting, interest without saving and reaping without sowing. This is a world without pride, a people without gratitude, and a soul that has never discovered the dignity and self-respect that comes from work and our own efforts.

They forget that every action and payment by government is the result of the enterprise, the risk taking and sweat of another. Every payment is the result of the efforts of hard working men and women who are advancing the shared hopes of the nation at the expense of their own.

Yes, the character of our country will always lend a hand and support those who carry more than their share of the vicissitudes of life. But our support must be a lift-up rather than a hand down. A lift-up must never be polluted by the stigma of shame, but equally, it must not take from either the giver or the recipient the incentive to make their own way in life.

Our world now ascribes virtue to those who receive a benefit rather than those who provide it. We must again give due honour to those who contribute.

The sweep of our lives and the sum of our lived experiences show that most of us are contributors as well as beneficiaries at some point in our lives. For all of us, there are times of fierce independence and other times, when help is needed and welcome, not just from government, but from our family, friends and neighbours as well.

As contributors, we recognise our blessings and opportunities. As beneficiaries, we must lean into a gratitude that frees the soul, rather than cultivate a sense of entitlement that is only satisfied by grumbling for more.

A stronger nation is the result of our combined efforts and contributions and it relies on a people who work.

Work is love made visible, it has dignity and it should strengthen the soul. Of course, there is struggle in work, and for some more struggle than others, but for most, the struggle should strengthen us and result in a healthy independence.

Work and family are at the heart of national life. Families provide us with love; and the efforts of our work, provide us with self-respect and dignity.

The sweat of our labour and pride in our own efforts, provide self-respect and dignity. This dignity is not the result of our social status or our income, but is the result of our honest and unceasing efforts.

When we deprive people of what they have earned through excessive taxation, or deprive them of an income because of a lack of a job, we destroy their dignity and this corrodes our families.

For governments to unduly burden those who work, is to take the reward from those who earned it. It is to mock effort, stymie initiative and incentive, and this in turn, slows the virtuous cycle that propels the progress of nations.

National life must not mock those who do the right thing. It must not despise them for making more in their life. How do we collectively excel, if we handicap those among us who thrive and succeed? Don't they by their efforts, create more opportunity and lift us as well? What happens if we quench the spirit which has propelled us for so long?

Our focus again must shift from meaningless debates about how we redistribute our existing national and personal income, to one that seeks to create wealth.

All too often, governments believe they know better than individuals and that they can manipulate and motivate individuals by using carrots and sticks.

Neither the dull hammer of disincentive nor the removal of weights that hold us back, can propel a nation or create a fierce independent spirit. Neither carrots nor sticks can spark enthusiasm, inspire new thinking, or improve our daily lot: only people can.

We either see individuals as incapable of making their own decisions or we see them as instruments for good in our world. When individuals are given responsibility and freed to lift their vision, they can and do create a more humane, and just world.

New laws do not change behaviours, unless they use the harshest measures. If governments could change the human condition then we would be rid of alcoholism, smoking, drug addiction, domestic violence and obesity. Along the way, we would also be rid of creativity, spontaneity, and humour, and we would ultimately reflect the "drab uniformity" that afflicts the totalitarian world.

Government might know more but it does not know better, it does not wake in the middle of the night for a crying baby, nor does it wait for elderly parents as they face their latest doctor's appointment. For all their virtues, governments have no soul, no life force, other than the very citizens they are meant to serve. The lesson of our times is to know that it is the virtue and spirit of the citizens and their willingness to stand by each other that sustains nations.

We must shift our focus from trust in government, and from the advancement of one group over another, to a trust in the values that have always undergirded progress: responsibility, honesty, thrift, faith and an honest day's work for an honest day's pay.

While there is truth in the words of William Ernest Henley, "I am the master of my fate, I am the captain of my soul", we are also knit to others. It is the knitting of people that creates families, communities and ultimately, nations.

An individual who does not belong, is an individual alone against the world, and a community that does not prize the individual is one where the light of individuality is snuffed out. Our national life must encourage government to do the essential things well, and have the confidence that individuals and 'little platoons' can manage the desirable things as well.

Economists have long warned of economic 'crowding out' where the resources and finances of government crowds out the opportunities of the private sector to grow and thrive, but we see in our modern world a new crowding out. This new crowding out is a mentality that robs people of the ability to make choices for their own lives. By taking more choices off the individual, we deny them the chance to become stronger, more aware and to make the best choices in their lives. Instead of success, they quietly brood about the failure that surrounds them and the inability for government to fix their problems.

We live in a time of unbridled want. Our leaders have created an expectation that every want will be met. Yet our wants are no vision for shared greatness. Our wants are demands that are withdrawals from the nation's stock of resources. Yes, many of our demands fulfil useful and valid purposes, many make our lives more secure, and our cities and suburbs more liveable and productive. Nevertheless, the culture of demand is eating us away.

We must look again to each other, rather than to government, because the best things are driven by individuals and communities and spring up from the bottom rather than be imposed from the top. Mostly, a better world is not the result of more government interventions and programs, rather it stems from the enterprise, self-motivation and drive of individuals that propels free societies and modern economies.

It is this ever-increasing demand and expectation for government that is not just crowding-out the enterprise of the individual, it is also destroying our faith in government.

A generation ago, interest in politics was low but trust in our leaders and institutions was high. Today, interest in politics is higher than ever and trust has never been as low. The pleasure that is often displayed by citizens when politicians are torn down is a reflection of the broken compact between the people and government. With each election, we expect more and inevitably we become disillusioned and disappointed.

This is the contradiction of modern life: we rage against politicians, impugn their motives, question their competency, at the same time as we ask them to do more and more. We seek government solutions to every human issue, and in so doing, demand standards they cannot meet and rob ourselves of the agency and urgency to improve our own lives.

Our future lies in a self-giving liberalism, where individuals can excel to the best of their ability, and where a civic unselfishness extends a helping hand to those that need it. These are not 'either or' options because together they reflect the true spirit of Australia.

The false wars
Great nations are founded on big, shared ideas. The American idea is "all men are created equal, that they are endowed by their Creator with certain unalienable Rights, that among these are Life, Liberty

and the Pursuit of Happiness". The British idea is of representative Parliamentary democracy, which is part of a body of institutions that give all individuals rights and a say. The French idea, revolutionary in its time is "liberty, equality and fraternity".

Australia has its own big idea. It is found in the Preamble of our Constitution "Whereas the people of New South Wales, Victoria, South Australia, Queensland, and Tasmania, humbly relying on the blessing of Almighty God, have agreed to unite in one indissoluble Federal Commonwealth". The big idea is that "the people have agreed to unite".

The idea that underpins our country is that we chose to become one people and as a *"common-wealth"* to share one indissoluble future. Our national idea is that we will stick by each other and with each other.

The 'common-wealth' is not a bank balance to deplete but an invitation to create and build a better future together.

That is why Menzies said the class war is so dangerous to Australia. The class war declares that we answer the question 'whose side are you on?' for almost every issue. It either seeks to strip those who have earned money of it, or it ignores the drumbeat of the poor for services and opportunity.

Menzies' question "what is the state but us?" is the defining question of our age.

The dividing of Australia for every debate into two camps weakens Australia. It turns our focus away from asking 'what can we contribute' to 'what we can get'.

In more recent times, this class war and its ugly twin 'the culture war', has been fuelled by interest groups, who are using the media tools of our age to weaponise anger. They have turned politics into sport and have accelerated the tribal view of supporting my party 'right or wrong'.

The end result of these professional lobbyist groups and the parties they represent is the professionalisation of division. Their robocalls, social media memes and videos seek to split Australian from Australian while at the same time they ask for another donation to help. In time, this leads to a ferocious escalation of division where ill-gotten attacks are answered by anger, a lack of civility and the absence of common courtesy.

These are false wars created by shadowy groups that take a *'win at all costs'* view of national life. In these wars, there are no casualties except an injured national spirit where 'all of us' are made weaker.

Menzies, using the words of St Paul, believed that we are "members of each other". He argued that we are part of a national body and we belong to each other.

The false wars that divide us every day, erode away the bonds between us. We are members of each other, be it as members of families, communities, and the nation. Tied to each other, we have a responsibility to each other.

We cannot care for each other, support each other and stand with each other, if most days we are at war with each other.

Though the unnecessary divisions and conflicts of our modern life lessen us all, it is the forgotten people who lose the most. By forcing the question 'whose side are you on', it is the forgotten people who straddle and tie the rich and poor together who suffer first, because it is the forgotten people who are working hard to make their way, but still aspiring for something better.

Critical to renewing our compact with each other is understanding that not everything in our national life is political. Decisions, mostly, are not made with bad intent or an absence of integrity.

Clickbait media and social media warriors seek to make everything political. This desperate attempt to turn everything into a contest and make every decision an opportunity to advance or hinder an opposing worldview is putting a strain on the social fabric.

Our national life is more than politics. It is Rotary and Surf Lifesaving; it is the faith of the churches and the dreaming of our Indigenous brethren; it is sculpture, architecture and arts; it the wonder of our ocean sunrise and the mystery of Uluru, and it is the countess, small kindnesses that we show to each other every day. This is the glory of our national life.

Modern Australia was not built on opinion, nor tweets or status updates, but on sacrifice, creativity and a grace to each other that reflects the original hope of Federation – of one people sharing one commonwealth.

In a world where tribalism is fracturing us into smaller and smaller groups, we must remind ourselves that true strength lies not in attacking others, but in showing to each other a generosity of spirit that allows us to walk in each other's shoes. We remember the words of a saint: in the essential things unity, in the important things diversity, in all things generosity.

The people who agreed to unite almost 120 years ago must rediscover a vision of our nation that sees unity in our diversity and strength in our differences – and we must work at it by giving each other the benefit of the doubt. As Menzies said: "there are many aspects in the world which appear superficially to be rough and tough, in which victory goes to the strongest, and the most enduring. No man was ever less strong, no man was ever less tough by treating with courtesy what others think or say, or do."

In this modern ecosystem which thrives on tribalism and division, leaders must fight for anyone who needs them, not just the subset or base who support them. True, the demand of modern politics requires that we defend 'the base', but our values demand that we fight for all who need us, not just those vocal few who are always in our corner. This is the way to advance liberalism rather than a narrow tribalism.

Our focus on enterprise should not be at the expense of understanding and seeking the advancement of those who are yet to prosper in our national life. Their slights and isolation are real. From the priority lines at airports to similar lines in our amusement parks and movie theatres, we are creating new silent divides that separate rich from those who are not. The forgotten people wait while others are ushered through. Little wonder the quiet resentments are building and Australians doubt if the professional and political class understand their daily struggles and slights.

While some focus on our different identities – be they race, creed, class, gender or sexual, and other focus on the political identities such of liberal, conservative, green, or that new term *'progressive'*, our focus must be on our shared identity as Australians and the ties that bind us.

We must continually ask ourselves: Are we freer? Are we stronger? Do we trust each other more? And are we focusing on the challenge of tomorrow instead of the enmities of today?

The politics of purpose

The forgotten people yearn for a return of national politics to the politics of purpose over the politics of the game.

Instead of being servants of the nation, our political class have become slaves to the game. As Menzies put it "how many hundreds of thousands of us are slaves to greed, to fear, to newspapers, to public opinion – represented by the accumulated views of our neighbours?"

To shift our focus from today to the future, requires us to forsake the modern shibboleth of polling. Polls tell us where we are, but they do not tell us what to do or where to go, because only leaders can do that.

Newspolls have made and undone more than one Australian prime minister in recent years and they have done their fair share of damage to the major parties. As Menzies said, "can you really believe that you can strike down the leader of a party, and do no injury to a party?"

It is worth asking the question: which Australian leader has lost more Newspolls than any other? The answer is not who you expect: it is our 25th Prime Minister, John Howard. From 1998 when Newspoll introduced the two-party preferred vote, until his eventual loss in 2007, John Howard lost 119 Newspolls or about 13 every year.

It reminds us that focus, patience, and perseverance are the best virtues for long-term political success. Polls can provide snapshots of the sentiment towards a government or leader but adherence to polls and the sugar hit of announcements, must not be a substitute for action based on the sure values of liberalism.

By focusing on the immediate, on daily announcements meant to keep the news-cycle and Newspolls, we allow ourselves to be drawn into a game where every day governments must solve new problems, make new announcements, and drive the political divide without ceasing.

All of this results in a political process that puts self over country, immediacy over the long-term, themeatics over nuance, and prioritises the game of politics over the great purpose of politics. It is to play the game of false wars and artificial divides that Menzies warned about so often.

As we reflect on the 75th anniversary of *The Forgotten People*, it is worth recalling just one of Bob Menzies forgotten people: Katherine Russell.

Katherine Russell was born in the later part of the 19th century and was the mother of nine children – seven sons and two daughters. She lost her husband to influenza in the 1920s and during the Great Depression she raised nine children single-handedly.

Katherine had a tough life but she was, by all accounts, one tough old battle-axe. In this politically correct world, I can write that because Katherine Russell was my great-grandmother.

After Mr Menzies declared war in 1939, Katherine Russell was given a badge – it was a silver badge with seven stars. The seven stars represented the seven sons she sent to fight for Australia.

She wore that badge every day throughout that war.

Near war's end, Katherine Russell was given another silver badge. This badge had two stars.

She wore this badge every day for the rest of her life.

The two stars – were for her sons: Andy and Charlie.

With victory in sight, Andy and Charlie were struck down. They were lost to the battle to defend freedom and human civilisation as we knew it.

That badge with two stars for her two sons, had two words: For Australia.

For Australia.

If there is a lesson for our times, it is that we must recapture the selfless values of those times.

We must find again a politics that puts country over self, long-term purpose over immediacy, that seeks to lead for all and not for some, unites rather than divides, and has at its heart the abiding values that defined Menzies' life and the party he bequeathed us.

2
FREEDOM OF SPEECH AND EXPRESSION

James Paterson

Robert Menzies probably would have found the threats to free speech in 2018 utterly bewildering.

He would have found it hard to envisage laws which exist to protect people from the giving and taking of offence, or from insults. He's unlikely to have foreseen large state bureaucracies charged with the investigation and resolution of these disagreements. He'd likely be shocked about the extent that public debate on legitimate public policy issues can be limited by the law. And he would almost certainly be troubled by the escalating demands for more legal controls on what people can say.

We know he was far from sanguine about the state of free speech in 1942. In his view, Australia fell "far short of really understanding or practising" this freedom. It's not much of a leap to imagine that Menzies would be horrified by the state of freedom of expression in Australia today.

There can be little doubt about the importance Menzies' placed on free speech. It was the first topic after the introduction in *The Forgotten People*, and he devoted two broadcasts to it. In the first federal platform of his new Liberal Party in 1946, freedom of speech was listed second, after parliamentary democracy. In his memoir in 1967, reflecting on the emphasis placed on the freedom to think and speak in his 1949 pre-election address, he describes these freedoms as the "heart of liberalism."

In *The Forgotten People* he characterises those who seek to unduly limit free speech in the harshest possible terms. Speaking in the midst of World War II, Menzies doesn't hesitate to label restrictions on free speech as "fascist", and regards the amount of free speech permitted as a measure of society's progress.

It's not difficult to predict what Menzies would have to say about the Human Rights Commission, section 18C of the *Racial Discrimination Act*, or those who seek to shut down debate today. Sadly, some of these restrictions have been put in place on the Liberal Party's watch, or failed to be repealed when we've had the opportunity to do so.

Australia today would benefit if Menzies' sophisticated approach to free speech was more widely reflected in our political class.

His understanding of free speech was both practical and philosophical. Like many free speech theorists, he believed free speech was good because it led to good outcomes. In his first broadcast he extolled the process of untrammelled debate as the best means of reaching the truth. He was humble enough to recognise that the truths of one era can become the false dogmas of the next – and that only the way to discover which was which is through unrestricted debate. He believed free speech to be an essential check on power, a tool for preserving democracy and a foe of authoritarianism.

But Menzies also believed in free speech because he believed it to be moral. He recognised the inseparability between the freedom to think and the freedom to speak, and it's close association with religious liberty. In his 1949 election speech, he refers to these freedoms as "the essence of man." In other words, intrinsic to humanity – the natural rights all free citizens possess, not merely means to an end. In *The Forgotten People* he praises John Stuart Mill's principled approach to individual liberties.

This is striking because in other respects Menzies is very much a product of his time, guided by a philosophy but suspicious of ideology and resolutely pragmatic. In an era when politicians prided themselves by contrasting their beliefs from the evil ideologies of socialism and fascism, his embrace of such a firm principle on free speech is unique.

Menzies' broad understanding of the merits of free speech is important because adopting only a consequentialist approach that we should allow free expression because it leads to the best outcomes is an extremely narrow platform from which to defend it. Opponents of free speech all too commonly point out that people can and do use this freedom to say things which are untrue, and perhaps even harmful. Exposing erroneous views in free debate is in fact crucial in the pursuit of truth, but it is too easy and dangerous to suggest, as some do, that we should shortcut this process by preventing them from being aired in the first place.

In contrast to many selective defenders of free speech, Menzies believed it is a freedom for everyone to enjoy equally. He showed remarkable liberal mindedness when he said in the Forgotten People broadcast:

> ... the whole essence of freedom is that it is freedom for others as well as ourselves: freedom for people who disagree with us as well as our supporters; freedom for minorities as well as for majorities.

He goes on to decry the "despotism of the majority" and highlights that it is minority opinion which most often needs the protection of free speech.

Menzies also knew that free speech is a freedom that is not dependent on your profession. In his second address on the topic, he argues that a journalist's "right of free speech and free thought is one that he shares with Mr Brown the butcher and Mr Robinson the bricklayer." It is a universal human right – not a special privilege for some.

There are many contemporary policy debates where this philosophy is tested. There is an increasing tendency to exempt journalists from certain laws and treat them as a special class of people who deserve unique protections. Anti-terrorism measures are one such example. The reasons for doing so are eminently sensible. But it is harder to defend restricting these exceptions to journalists only, particularly in an age where the boundaries of journalism are becoming blurred and the barriers to citizens participating in public debate are falling. If a limitation on freedom is too much for journalists, perhaps it's too much for all of us.

In an era where participants in public debate are highly sensitive to criticism, we can draw two important lessons from Menzies. Like all political leaders, he received his fair share of criticism from the media. At times he makes clear he felt some of it was unwarranted and unfair. But even amidst that he never wavered in his defence of the media's duty to hold him and his contemporaries to account. Nor did he propose draconian legislation in response.

Secondly, Menzies never fell into the increasingly common modern trap of claiming that mere criticism of ones ideas somehow constitutes an impermissible limitation on free speech. Criticism is not censorship. Bad ideas should be exposed to tough public scrutiny. As he argues in *The Forgotten People*, "it is a poorly founded or weakly held belief which cannot resist the onset of another man's critical mind."

Some on the centre right of Australian politics today are too quick to deploy the political correctness defence when all that has happened is that someone's speech has been criticised. When the left so often and so successfully play the victim card in public debate it is tempting for liberals and conservatives to occasionally do the same – but it is a dangerous trend for two reasons.

Firstly, the most serious restrictions on free speech are those put in place by the state. And there are more than enough of them at the state and federal level for us to worry about before we start worrying about more trivial issues. Perhaps when 18C is repealed and no state has laws like Tasmania's radical anti-discrimination statute, we can move on to lower-order restrictions.

Secondly, at the more extreme end, political correctness can be a serious problem. When people are hounded out of their jobs in private companies for having views that only mildly differ from the zeitgeist of the day, public debate is unquestionably poorer for it. Personal attacks launched with the aim of totally stifling a legitimate point of view in the public square should never be tolerated. Ludicrous boycotts that aim to deny there are debates to be had at all must be opposed.

But if we cry wolf every time someone is simply called out for their views, we'll have no credibility opposing these more militant forms of political correctness.

While Menzies would despair at how much free speech has been restricted in our modern age, he would probably also be taken aback by the range and tone of speech that takes place in modern Australia. Since his time, there has unquestionably been a decline in our ability as a society to conduct public debate in a good spirit, to disagree without being disagreeable. Menzies' harshest critics would surely acknowledge the warmth and generosity of spirit in which he conducted himself even amid fraught and challenging public disputes.

Part of this decline stems from technological change. The rise of social media has inevitably caused the decline of the old gatekeepers to public debate – such as newspaper editors, radio and television journalists. Where once all public discussion was filtered through them, now any individual can access the public square. There are many benefits from this. For one, it is much more democratic. But it has undoubtedly contributed to the coarsening of public discussion.

As Liberals who seek to uphold Menzies' legacy, we have an obligation to not just live up to the philosophical standard he set, but do so with the class and dignity that he demonstrated. That means conducting ourselves well in public debate, and calling out those who fail to. While we may not be able to – and certainly don't wish to – control how others participate in public forums, we can and should set an example of how civil discourse can be conducted. If we don't do so we invite more of the regulation we detest.

While Menzies was a staunch defender of free speech, he didn't hold a caricatured absolutist view of it. He accepted two main limitations on it. He defended the need for censorship in a time of war as a necessary evil, although he was anxious that it did not go too far.

Speaking in the House of Representatives shortly after he had declared Australia was at War in September 1939, he spoke powerfully about the need to preserve our freedoms at home while we were at war to defend those same freedoms abroad:

> Our institutions of parliament, and of liberal thought, free speech, and free criticism, must go on. It would be a tragedy if we found that we had fought for freedom and fair play and the value of the individual human soul, and won the war only to lose the things we were fighting for.

Critics of Menzies sometimes argue that his later attempt to ban the Communist Party conflicted with this fine sentiment, and was even hypocritical given his defence of free speech. Whatever we think of the merits of his efforts to do so, this is a harsh judgement. Menzies never sought to ban Communist speech or Communist ideas, but he certainly believed that a Communist organisation should not be permitted to exist in Australia during the Cold War. He and many of his contemporaries regarded the Communist Party in much the same way we today regard modern terrorist organisations, which we rightly ban.

Menzies was also comfortable with defamation as a reasonable limitation on what could be said. In Menzies time defamation law was used differently to how it often is today. Prominent public figures, like politicians, did not routinely resort to it to shut down criticism. There is no record of Menzies ever having sued someone personally for defamation. He seemed to think that such criticism came with the territory, and perhaps that people with a public platform like himself already had ample opportunity to correct the record and respond accordingly without recourse to the courts.

There's no question that in Australia today, defamation is a threat to free speech. While there remains a strong theoretical need to protect the reputations of people who would have no other means of doing so, it is now routinely used by those best placed to defend themselves from criticism they don't like. Senior political leaders, entertainers, prominent business figures, and others with enviable access to a public megaphone should not be resorting to the law except in the most egregious cases. This is particularly important in an age where a defamation lawsuit – successful or not – represents a far greater threat to the financial viability of media organisations than it once did.

As custodians of Menzies' legacy today, the Liberal Party must seize every opportunity to uphold the political value arguably closest to Menzies' heart. The Liberal Party is at its best when it stands up for free speech – especially when doing so is politically tough. When we demonstrate we can be relied on to defend this core ideal, our supporters are reassured we are and remain the Party of values they want us to be.

3
FREEDOM OF WORSHIP

Julian Leeser

I write this as I watch my first-born child peacefully sleep in his hospital crib.

James Samuel John Leeser bears the name of his grandfather and two of his great grandfathers; and he carries Joanna and my greatest hopes.

We have given him names of his forebears not just because, according to tradition, we honour our grandparents but because we want him to know that his story does not just start with him, or with us, but that he is a link in a chain to a family, a society and a set of values and traditions.

He was born at the Sydney Adventist Hospital, a hospital whose staff are called to care in the Christian Adventist Tradition, a people who take their Sabbath seriously.

To any parent their child is precious. Jo and I want for James the same thing that other parents want for their children. To have a long, happy, healthy and fulfilling life full of opportunity and free of any discrimination that would prevent him from being himself.

James is a seventh generation Australian. He is inheriting a country from his parents who have inherited from their parents and so on across the generations.

I want James to understand what is uniquely good about this land and to understand his duty to preserve the inheritance he has had from his parents as I have from mine.

I also want James to understand the particular perspective of being a Jewish Australian – a religious minority which has never numbered more than one percent of the population – in a land which has been, almost uniquely in human history, good to the Jewish people.

Across those seven generations some parts of my family came to try their luck in a new land while other parts of the family came to Australia to escape religious persecution from the pogroms and the Holocaust to the security of Australia.

With each generation, that faith ebbed and flowed, as different ancestors reflected on what it meant to be Jewish in their times. Some were religious, some less so and that choice will be before James it was before them. Just like James' own parents, his ancestors weren't perfect, but as I have discovered, their journeys can give strength to face your own tests and trials.

One of the things that makes me proud of Australia is that it has been a religiously tolerant land where people can freely practise their faith.

The measure of a truly free society is how it treats its minorities. Does it grant them full citizenship rights or does it provide for discriminatory laws?

In his own day Menzies was always as concerned about minority rights as he was majority rights, Menzies said that "although the essence of democracy is that the majority shall rule, democracy can never be the real instrument of freedom unless its majorities are constantly tender for the rights of their minorities."

For people of faith their particular faith is fundamental to who they are and how they see the world. For people of faith the idea that a tradition or a set of beliefs is ordained by God (or whatever Supreme Being they might believe in) is not like an ordinary belief. It is the most fundamental of beliefs.

Freedom of Worship

The right to practise your faith according to its traditions, customs and beliefs is fundamental to a believer's very existence. That is why true believers seek to leave countries where people are not able to freely exercise their religious beliefs or worse still are persecuted for it.

Australia has never been that sort of a country.

Throughout history in Europe, Africa and the Middle East, Jews have been persecuted for their faith – forced to convert, forced to choose to deny their beliefs, or forced to renounce God. They have been murdered because their religious beliefs, practices and laws were different.

But in Australia Jews have always been able to be that which they are called upon to be, a light unto the nations, to perform the *mitzvot* or good deeds according to the Law of Moses.

In Jeremiah we are told to "pray for the peace of the city for if it prospers so to shall you prosper".

And so into the bargain of practising their faith Jews have contributed to Australia vastly beyond their tiny numbers.

Right from the start Australia has been a religiously diverse land. On the first fleet there were a dozen Jewish convicts.

No office has ever been barred to Jews in Australia. This is the country of Sir John Monash and Sir Isaac Isaacs.

Jews have had the freedom to practise their faith almost right from the get-go.

There has never been any exclusion of Jews from assuming full civil office in this land. Four years before Jews were admitted to the British Parliament Sir Saul Samuel was elected to the NSW Legislative Council in 1854. In 1860 he became possibly the first Jew in the British Empire to become a minister of the Crown.

In colonial times Vaiben Solomon was Premier of South Australia and with Isaacs and Elias Solomon the three were members of the first Commonwealth Parliament. It is with some considerable pride that I am today one of six Jewish members of the Commonwealth Parliament.

As an Australian James will meet many people of different faiths and will have the opportunity to experience the customs and ceremonies of faith communities which are not his own.

Australia is a country which has at its foundation the Judeo-Christian tradition which has the been the font of liberalism with two notions at its core. First, that life is a sacred gift from God and second, that all human beings, whoever we are, are created in the image and likeness of God and that therefore all human beings are deserving of equal dignity. The sanctity of life and the dignity of the human person form the touch stone of liberalism's focus on the individual over the collective and the importance of preserving life as a national policy goal.

James was born into a society which is predominantly, at least nominally, Christian which has a full range of Eastern and Western Churches – Catholic and Protestant, Pentecostal and Orthodox.

He will also have the chance to meet Australians who make up the 10 percent of our population who adhere to non-Christian religions.

From European settlement until 1981 Judaism was the major non-Christian denomination in Australia. But since that time, the number of Muslims, Buddhists, Hindus and Sikhs has overtaken the number of Jews in this country.

The religious diversity of Australia means that Australians from every faith background and no faith background have the chance to share their traditions with others. This is no threatening thing.

For those people who are comfortable in their own faith tradition engaging with other traditions can be a way of strengthening belief, understanding and loyalty to your own tradition.

Freedom of Worship

My parents chose to send me to an Anglican school because they wanted me to be part of the mainstream of society and to understand Australia's dominant Christian tradition, its theology, its beliefs and its culture.

But they also instilled in me a sense that while we should respect Christianity, our faith was different. This was instilled in me when unlike my class mates on Friday night I was at home for Shabbat dinners, we attended synagogue on a Friday night and Saturday, not a Sunday. And every week I would attend classes in Hebrew and Jewish studies to prepare me for my bar mitzvah.

These were not things most of my other classmates had to do.

But having my own faith tradition that was different from the other boys was not a negative it was a positive. I understood their tradition and could tell them some of mine.

Years later prior to entering the Parliament, I spent the best four years working for Australian Catholic University where I not only spent time thinking about education policy but about the future of the Church in Australia and its place in our national life more broadly.

I also had the privilege of serving on the board of Mercy Health – a large Catholic Health organisation run by the Sisters of Mercy. When I was asked to serve on the Board by their Executive Chairman Julien O'Connell I had to tell Julien that I am not a Catholic but a Jew just in case being of the Catholic faith was a precondition for serving on the board. Julian paused and said. "That's funny I think we had a Jewish bloke involved in the organisation once you might have heard of him his name was Jesus Christ!" That was typical of Julien's humour but it is also typical of the openness of the Australian Catholic Church.

While Catholicism is not my faith tradition, in order to support the mission of the University I would often attend Mass celebrated by the resident university priest Fr Anthony Casamento csma. There is something beautiful about sitting quietly, reflecting, watching people of deep faith observe the rituals and hearing the biblical readings some from my own bible and some from the New Testament and reflecting on what that wisdom means for us. Rituals of this sort provide clarity and calm in what can often be a chaotic world.

My best friend Shahan Ahmed and I were at high school and law school together. Our friendship is born of our shared experience. Shahan is a Muslim. His father Salah was a distinguished legal academic who taught contract law to a generation of students at UNSW. He is also an expert in Islamic law. Shahan's grandfather had been the first Attorney General of Bangladesh. Shahan now follows the family tradition and has built a successful practice at the NSW Bar. Shahan has shared Passover with us and we have shared Eid with him. I have learnt something of Islam from him and he has learnt something of Judaism from me. These are the bonds that make Australia stronger.

It says something good about Australia that a Jewish boy could be educated by Anglicans, work for the largest mission of the Catholic Church and have a best friend who is a Muslim.

That is not to say people of faith have always got along in Australia.

Until the early 1970s there was a sectarian divide between protestants and Catholics it was a divide that was so distinct that when Jim Spielman the future Chief Justice of NSW joined the other major political party he was asked "are you a protestant or a Catholic?" To which he replied "I am a Jew" his interlocutor continued "Yes but are you a protestant Jew or a Catholic Jew?"

It says something about Menzies – in fact it defines Menzies as a liberal in my view – that he never brought into the sectarian debate although there would have been plenty of votes in doing so. Menzies could boast that "I had never lent myself to any bitter disputes between people on the basis of their religion"

Menzies was a proud Presbyterian Scot but he actively rejected sectarianism and went further and became the first national political leader to provide financial assistance to the Catholic School system. In fact, he was so concerned to create equality of educational opportunity regardless of the religious tradition of the school that he told an audience in 1964

> ... there are those who say, "you can't fail to discriminate between Protestant and Catholic schools". And the answer is that if I had to do that I would not want to be in public life.

Today while more than two-thirds of Australians register themselves as adherents to one or other faith, the number of Australians with any sort of religious literacy is declining.

The public conversation about religion is not assisted by simplifications of religious doctrines and the assumption by some in the media that religious leaders are either paedophiles, terrorists or obsessed with some else's sex life.

Religion is being delegitimised by those who believe that it is based on superstitions not science, and at worst, pits competing minorities against each other and calls for protections to be able to discriminate against people who are not part of 'the club'.

True, some of our religious institutions have suffered from poor leadership and moral corruption and as a newer generation of leaders has arisen they are not always quick to see that religions are operating in a more hostile public environment. It is a rare politician or journalist who will profess their faith in public and or quote from the Bible. Christianity which has been the dominant religion in Australia since European Settlement has been more in the gun than other faiths and we have seen Christian religious practices and preferences subjected to challenges in the State Courts.

The population seems to be unsympathetic to providing protections for religious freedom where that means that the practice they are looking to protect is out of step with the community and seeks to discriminate against others. And yet to people of faith these beliefs and actions are fundamental to their conception of themselves.

But somehow religion survives as Lord Jonathan Sacks, the former Chief Rabbi in the commonwealth reminds us:

> Religion survives because it answers three questions that every reflective person must ask. Who am I? Why am I here? How then shall I live? We will always ask those three questions because *homo sapiens* is the meaning-seeking animal, and religion has always been our greatest heritage of meaning...We stand to lose a great deal if we lose religious faith. We will lose our Western sense of human dignity. I think we will lose our Western sense of a free society. I think we will lose our understanding of moral responsibility. I think we will lose the concept of a sacred relationship, particularly that of marriage, and we will lose our concept of a meaningful life. I think that religious belief is fundamental to Western civilisation and we will lose the very heart of it if we lose our faith ...
>
> I once defined faith as the redemption of solitude. It sanctifies relationships, builds communities, and turns our gaze outward from self to other, giving emotional resonance to altruism and energising the better angels of our nature. These are some of the gifts of our encounter with transcendence, and whether it is love of humanity that leads to the love of God or the other way round, it remains the necessary gravitational force that keeps us,

each, from spinning off into independent orbits, binding us instead into the myriad forms of collective beatitude.

A society without faith is like one without art, music, beauty or grace, and no society without faith can endure for long.

I believe religion has a particular role to play in the world today. The search for meaning in people's lives has never been greater than it is today. We see it in the rise of youth suicides, we see it in the rise of secular substitutes for faith communities, we see it in the disaffection of young people and in some segments of society the attraction of radical Islam. In this context strong, welcoming, confident, faith communities have an important voice that needs to be heard more in the public square.

Menzies remarks that religion constantly reminds Australians that "however clever he may be he is not his own maker, however self-confident he may think he is, he is living in a world not created by him, that he has responsibilities, that he has great inheritances, that he is responsible in his own proper fashion for the people who come after him… a background of faith, a background of humility.. must be the inevitable products of religious belief."

4
FREEDOM FROM WANT

Ken Wyatt

Freedom from want is something most Australians take for granted. We're confident there will be food on the table, clothing, a bed to sleep in, a roof over our head and that the trappings of everyday life will be there to be enjoyed.

Concern about freedom from want is an alien concept for the majority of us. We have prospered as a nation, enjoying a standard of living envied by many, one that continues to draw eager migrants from almost every corner of the world.

But for a significant number of our First Nations peoples and other Australian families facing poverty or homelessness, this is not the norm as they endure a life of hardship.

When I was a child growing up in Western Australia's vast Wheatbelt, I experienced many instances of living from week to week and day to day.

Time and time again I thought of a life where my father, mother, brothers and sisters and I could live without being hungry, having the basic things in life that it seemed every other family enjoyed.

Cool drinks, biscuits, cake, steak, new clothes and having toys were rare experiences. Instead damper, kangaroo, dripping, lambs fry and mutton flaps were staple foods, along with Weet-Bix.

We kids yearned for Dad's payday because that's when we sometimes received things that other kids had, such as lollies and fruit, which we relished.

My father worked hard on the railways and did weekend jobs, too, to provide for my Mum and all eight of us children but it was never enough to fully meet our needs.

I distinctly remember the Christmas when my mother quietly explained to us that there would be no presents from Santa Claus because he couldn't afford to bring us anything.

At the time, my father had been off work for three months, recovering from complication from a hernia operation. Social security was for a defined period and that had long run out, so things were especially tough.

We ate two meals a day and at lunch time we came home to have damper and jam. We also survived on cornflour custard and the rabbits I caught.

As children, we accepted the fact that Father Christmas would not be coming to us.

On 24 December, though, there came a knock on the door and I went to see who it was.

Outside was a man, who asked if Mum or Dad was home, so I yelled out to my father, telling him there was someone out the front, wanting to see him.

When my father came to the door the man introduced himself and said that a trailer had been delivered to his place by mistake and that it was for us.

We all followed my father outside, to see a large box trailer, covered by a tarpaulin. On two sides it had signs, with the words "The Wyatt family, 51 Goyder Street, Corrigin."

He pulled the tarpaulin back, revealing generous hampers of food, Mickey Mouseketeers stools and what seemed like hundreds of smaller presents wrapped in bright paper and tinsel, along with many bottles of cool drinks.

This extraordinary gesture made that Christmas one I will never forget.

The presents were gratefully unwrapped but, looking back amost 60 years, it was the joy of such unexpected generosity that has proved the most enduring gift.

That memory remains with me and with my siblings, as powerful reminder of how important giving is, how it offers love, hope and certainty.

Over time, the concept of freedom from want has been an elusive dream that speaks to so many families and First Nations Australians, in so many aspects of their daily lives.

It is about alleviating the cruelty of racism, the opportunity to have a healthy birth and future, access to basic health services and care, education to acquire the knowledge and skills to succeed in life, and being able to enjoy social success, social justice and inclusion.

I felt a soaring sense of satisfaction – almost disbelief – when I was able to take my place in the House of Representatives and in my first speech, say "I stand as an equal". I had achieved a dream to be a member of a great institution enshrined in the Constitution – the Australian Parliament.

Yet I know what it's like to be denigrated for my race, to be told to leave school and to get a job on a farm, because "Aboriginal kids don't succeed, you all go on walkabout".

I have lived through poverty and hunger more times as a child than I wish to remember. I recall the pain, and the shame, of not being able to go to the local doctor because my Mum and Dad couldn't afford to pay.

I'm where I am now because of my loving parents, who pushed and encouraged my siblings and me, but there were other people and organisations who believed in me and helped me embrace pathways to opportunity.

In particular, there was support from the Rotary Club of Corrigin, the local branch of the Country Women's Association, plus businessman Dean Rundle and school principal Allan Jones, who understood the critical importance of education and were determined to help me achieve this.

As I reached my teens during the 1960s, I was able to attend a boarding school, during which time I briefly encountered the impressive figure of Sir Robert Menzies at an event in Forrest Place, outside the Perth GPO.

Looking back at that time of change – just before the 1967 referendum – and further back, to Menzies' original Forgotten People, I find his foresight compelling.

During the early 1940s, he focused on Australians who didn't have a voice, who were often forgotten in the context of many of the policies that the Australian Government had implemented.

Recently, I saw some precious documents at Perth's Berndt Museum of Anthropology and, sifting through a number of the articles from 1967, I was overwhelmed by déjà vu, around issues that have been raised in the past and still have not been adequately addressed.

In cyclic terms, we see protests and the raising of voices in frustration at not being able to exercise enough influence on political and social policies and agendas.

If we take the principle of Menzies' work, then the forgotten people are those who sit within each community, the people who feel powerless to exercise influence or change the feelings of futility they have.

So, the term forgotten people is probably more apt for Aboriginal and Torres Strait Islander people than for just about any other section of Australian society.

I vividly recall a conversation I had when many Vietnamese

refugees were settling in Australia as refugees, a discussion about the acceptance of one community against another. In that dinner table discussion, a person commented that he would rather accept Vietnamese refugees as neighbours, than have Aboriginal people living next door. In his mind, the Vietnamese refugees would assimilate better than Australia's First Peoples.

What he lost sight of was the fact that the First Nations people have for so long been dispossessed in so many ways, on so many fronts, to the extent that States and Territories legislated under various policies and approaches to control their lives.

If we look at the history of many country centres, including where I grew up, Aboriginal people were put on reserves and weren't allowed into town. They weren't exactly forgotten people but they were isolated and there were strict controls over them.

And so the context of history for forgotten Aboriginal and Torres Strait Islander Australians has permeated through every decade and even today – when we consider the gaps in health, in education, in infrastructure and housing – the disparity is still stark.

Opportunity is generated firstly by those who wish to seize it but, equally, that opportunity won't prevail if there is a view that someone is not worthy of consideration.

I think of the journey that I have had and the people who believed in me and helped create opportunities. I know, too, there were many of my young Aboriginal colleagues who never received those chances.

Today, the levels of disparity across such a geographically diverse nation as ours require all three tiers of government, non-government organisations and First Nations families, Elders, mothers and fathers, to work together to continue turning around the current situation.

I recall a speech United Nations Secretary General Ban Ki-moon delivered in 2015, in which he stated: "Today's extraordinary challenges can be seen and addressed through the four lenses of freedom: Freedom of expression, freedom of worship, freedom from want and freedom from fear."

His speech drew on the 1941 State of the Nation address by US President Franklin D. Roosevelt, in which he expressed his view on the four fundamental rights that he believed the world should universally embrace.

Earlier in his first term he had shared his concern that American democracy could not survive if one-third of the nation were ill-housed, ill-clothed and ill-fed.

He saw the need to address freedom from want because he believed that the levels of poverty and hardship, currency disruption, unemployment and financial desperation allowed dictators like Adolf Hitler to rise to power.

Ban Ki-moon went on to say that Human Rights Day needed a more concentrated and global approach to the timeless principle which he framed against contemporary global challenges facing member Nations. He couched freedom from want accordingly.

Freedom from want remains a deeply relevant challenge. World leaders adopted the 2003 Agenda for Sustainable Development with the aim of ending poverty and enabling all people to live in dignity on a peaceful, healthy planet.

Now we must do everything possible to realise this vision.

Unless freedom from want is the underpinning principle of widespread reform in Australia, then the alternatives that may evolve will be far more challenging than Closing the Gap.

Already, some of our young First Nations people are being drawn into groups that are not conducive to a civil and orderly society.

Sadly, I still meet families in my electorate of Hasluck and in some Aboriginal communities who desire a better future but feel a sense of frustration, futility and anger that generates a sense that "nothing will ever get better".

To some Aboriginal people, Closing the Gap is "gammon" – there is no genuine sense of seeing change for the community as a whole, even though there are now so many examples of individuals and groups succeeding.

Instead, these people under pressure – the families and communities who do not have freedom from want – are often overwhelmed by health and education targets not being met, high suicide rates, chronic conditions and housing challenges.

All these areas of concern need firm approaches that demand individual, family and community involvement and responsibility, but built on national understanding of, and respect for, the longest continuous culture on Earth.

The twinkling lights include health, education and housing programs driven from the family level upwards, plus the thousands of younger Aboriginal and Torres Strait Islander people now grasping training, business and professional opportunities to expand the economic base for their families, communities and the nation.

To create an Australia that truly addresses freedom from want requires mutual cultural respect, coupled with strong leadership at all levels.

The message behind Menzies' Forgotten People rings true today: That we must turn our eyes, hearts and minds to all of Australia's forgotten peoples, to work and walk together with them and support them in their quest for a strong voice and an ever stronger contribution to our nation's future.

5
FREEDOM FROM FEAR

Nick Cater

Long after the war was over, Robert Menzies was to declare that a government's most important task was to preserve the economic freedom that allows individuals and businesses to thrive. Menzies' priorities were ordered very differently in July 1942 when he delivered two radio addresses on the topic of Freedom from Fear.

He begins with a reminder that the government's most important task was to protect its citizens. Germany and Japan, "the arch lawbreakers, the dark angels of fear", must be defeated, and defeated absolutely, "if honest men are to sleep quietly in their beds". By that stage of the war, seven months after the entry of the United States, there could be no possibility of a negotiated peace. Germany must be taught "that war does not pay; that crime leads to punishment; that the rights of the world are greater than those of the German Empire."

Yet Menzies does not dwell on that theme for long, conscious perhaps that few listeners would need to be persuaded of the enemy's malignance. The war had already arrived on Australian soil; the Brisbane line was in place to stop a southward invasion by the Japanese, and air and sea defences were on alert in eastern capitals. Besides, Menzies seldom restricted his addresses to a single thought and on this occasion, like any seasoned politician, he decided to interpret the topic widely. In the second of the two addresses, he shifts the focus to domestic politics, making some profound observations about fear mongering and populism and appealing for conviction and courage, themes to which he frequently returned in post-war speeches.

The fears that gripped Australians in the middle of a war that posed an existential threat to freedom itself were real and justified. They arguably resonate more strongly today than they would have in the 1950s when Menzies gave prominence to economic freedom. Nobody could accuse Menzies of taking the threats to liberty posed by communism lightly. The Cold War was not fought on Australian soil, however, at least not in a physical sense, unlike the war against Islamist ideologues we are fighting today.

Freedom from fear is today under explicit assault from terrorism and the battle is very clearly being fought on our shores. The Brisbane line has been redrawn in the heart of our cities, manifest in the bollards under construction in public places and the controversial eyesore of a fence around Parliament House in Canberra. The sight of military style police armed with machine guns no longer shocks us in airports and around public buildings, even though it should, for they are standing the last line of the defence of liberty.

It is difficult to argue with Malcolm Turnbull's assertion that "the primary duty of every government, state or federal, is to protect the safety of citizens", but that doesn't stop some trying. Some would argue that the state's duty of care extends beyond its own citizens to the population of the world and, indeed, the preservation of the planet. Yet that was decidedly not Menzies' view as he explored the failings of the League of Nations, a post-World War I institution that emerged from the same supra-national yearning that later gave birth to the United Nations in 1945. The League's fundamental weakness was the understandable reluctance of its members to surrender sovereignty. Citizens may be willing to surrender their own absolute individual sovereignty in favour of the greater sovereignty of the State and security and freedom that would follow. To expect them to surrender their sovereignty in obedience to international law was, however, in Menzies' view fanciful.

> Would you, if you were in charge of our affairs at the end of the war, be willing for us to enter a League of Nations which was a sort of super-State and which could give us orders? ... Our deep-seated national instincts, traditions, may make it impossible.

Menzies would undoubtedly have been in favour of Brexit. His 1942 address foreshadows the contradictions at the heart of the United Nations and the European Union, a body to which he later expressly objected.

To test the wisdom of Menzies' aversion to supranationalism, let us imagine an Australia in which his view had held sway. There would be no *Race Relations Act* and no Australian Human Rights Commission, since under the constitution, the Commonwealth would have no jurisdiction over matters of discrimination outside federal territories. The commonwealth's authority comes from its obligation to enforce international treaties and is exercised under section 51 (xxix) of the Constitution which relates to external affairs. Hence an international treaty, enforced by a compliant federal government, usurps the sovereignty of state governments granted to them by the people in a manner not envisaged by those who drafted the Constitution.

Menzies with his knowledge of both constitutional law and the wily skills of government foresaw this development, and rejected calls for Australia to sign the United Nations Declaration on the Elimination of All Forms of Racial Discrimination (1963). In retirement, Menzies was to explain his objection writing: "The external affairs power was never designed to be an internal affairs power or to alter the distribution of power between the

Commonwealth and the States." Nevertheless, in April 1966, four months after Menzies' retirement from parliament, his successor Harold Holt signed the declaration opening the way for the Whitlam government's Racial Discrimination Act in 1975 and the controversial clause 18C included in the racial vilification amendments introduced by the Keating government two decades later.

Freedom from fear surely includes the expectation that one will not face persecution by the institutions of one's own state. Yet persecution was exactly what The Australian's cartoonist Bill Leak felt when the AHRC pursued a case against him based on a flimsy claim that he had drawn a cartoon that might "offend, insult, humiliate or intimidate" indigenous Australians. In the foreword to a book of cartoons launched two days before his untimely death Leak wrote:

> It was a case of an instrument of the state turning its goon squad onto one its own citizens in a brutal, no-hold barred attempt to shut him up. And if that's not a clear sign we're on the slippery slope to totalitarianism I don't know what is.

Menzies' warnings about surrendered sovereignty are a neat segue into his second address of freedom from fear which switches focus from the international sphere to the domestic. Fear was such a potent instrument in domestic policy, Menzies argued, that it was arguably the most significant of all the emotions on the field of politics, ripe for exploitation in dictatorships. "When Hitler set up his dictatorship he saw at once that nothing sustains a dictatorship as does fear," said Menzies. "Frightened people are much more pliant instruments and much readier receptacles for notions of hatred and revenge than people who move and have their beings in the brave daylight of a free mind."

Democracies are not immune to the politics of fear, he suggests asking rhetorically "must we not admit that fear colours our political and social life profoundly?" We think we know where he is heading; towards condemnation of the dark art of fear mongering as a political tactic. At first Menzies chooses to censure not the politicians but the populace for encouraging the practice:

> Every student of political history knows that there have been political elections in Australia won by an appeal to greed and others won by an appeal to fear. And the fact that they were won shows that the politicians did not misjudge the people.

Then, with a dexterous narrational twist, he lashes his tongue at his own profession, not for manufacturing fear but for succumbing to it.

He notes the rise of pressure politics, and the use of organised letter-writing campaigns aimed at parliamentarians. In reality they are little more than "an endeavour to exploit the instinct of fear" in the expectation that the recipient "will be sufficiently spineless to abandon his own reasoned convictions for fear of losing his seat in Parliament."

The politics of conviction, supported by an intelligent assessment of the facts, was a familiar theme in Menzies' writings and speeches for the best part of half a century. "If I have honestly and thoughtfully arrived at a certain conclusion on a public question and my electors disagree with me, my first duty is to endeavour to persuade them that my view is right," he says. "If I fail in this, my second duty will be to accept the electoral consequences and not to run away from them. Fear can never be a proper or useful ingredient in those mutual relations of respect and goodwill which ought to exist between the elector and the elected."

Giving way to a temporary clamour by thousands of people who lacked information and may not have thought the issue through was to surrender to populism. "Nothing can be worse for democracy than to adopt the practice of permitting knowledge to be overthrown by ignorance."

Finally, Menzies returns to the virtue of courage and the dangers of its absence not just from politics but from business and social life. Fear "too often restrains experiment and keeps us from innovations which might benefit us enormously," he says. "It is the fear of knowledge which prevents so many of us from really using our minds, and which makes so many of us ready slaves to cheap and silly slogans and catch-cries." Fear leads us "to yearn for… some safe billet from which risk and its twin brother enterprise are alike abolished."

Yielding to fear leads to "hysteria and greed and burden-dodging."

By the end of the address, Menzies' radio audience, listening in on a winter's night in wartime more than three years away from victory, might have wondered whether they had not listened to a political address but a sermon. Fear cannot be overcome by simply making the outside world a safer place; the will to defeat it must come from within.

Like every human right, freedom from fear is attached to human responsibilities. To obtain it, Menzies concludes, "we shall need to prosecute to victory not only our war against Germany and Japan, but a constant war against ourselves."

6
EMPIRE CONTROL OF AN EMPIRE WAR

Tony Abbott

In January 1942, not long before the fall of Singapore, Bob Menzies broadcast about the working relationship that the Australian government had with the British one and how the strategic intimacy between our two countries was vital for the success of the war effort. Although Britain and Australia, merely as a function of geography, had different strategic priorities, there's no doubt that we had the same values and the same overall interests. As in the Great War before it and as in the current conflict in the Middle East, between the Western allies World War Two was a common struggle; and a common struggle, as Menzies recognised, is best conducted with the closest possible collegiality.

Menzies detailed the multitude of ways in which the British and Australian establishments interacted to maintain a common approach to the war that threatened all of us: high commissioners conferred with senior officials almost daily; there were regular confidential cables; and there were semi-annual ministerial and prime ministerial delegations to London. The British Empire executive sitting in London that Menzies called for in that broadcast was as impractical in early 1942 as something similar would be today because national leaders cannot be away from home for extended periods, even in wartime. Yet his fundamental point about the need for confidentiality, collegiality and collaboration between like-minded allies is as correct today as it was then. If Australia is to be secure, and if the world's well-being is to be advanced, then the countries that are most committed to universal respect and to the like-freedom-of-all need to work together in every possible way.

So many of the issues that our country faces have an important international dimension: our safety, for instance, means reducing the impact of global jihadism; our prosperity, for instance, requires reducing trade barriers so that there's more potential to make the best use of people's talents. As the world becomes more ever-more-interconnected, the impact upon us of overseas events and policies pursued abroad will continue to escalate.

In his 1942 broadcast, Menzies observed that high level "repeated, regular, personal contacts have been the best possible things" for advancing the mutual interests of like-minded nations. Australia's capacity to respond to the 2014 MH17 atrocity is a contemporary example of the importance of personal contact. My previous meetings with the Dutch Prime Minister at that year's Davos conference and with the Ukrainian President just six weeks earlier at the 70th anniversary of D-Day meant that these leaders didn't have to be "cold-called" to help to arrange an effective response to the killing of almost 300 people (including 39 Australians) by Russian-backed rebels.

If Australia is to expect goodwill and a disposition to help from others, it's vital that this be our own approach too. In every country, the job of government is to wrestle with the most difficult and intractable problems; so the last thing that national leaders want, on top of all their existing challenges, is avoidable grief from the leaders of other countries. I tried to make it my rule as prime minister to start relations with other leaders by finding a way to be helpful; even if it were only saying something that was true and that they would want to hear.

Hence, I declared that Indonesia was (with India) the world's emerging democratic superpower and that size, proximity and potential made it our most important relationship. I apologised to the Malaysian Prime Minister for the way his country had been dragged into our domestic politics of border protection. I congratulated Japan for being an exemplary global citizen since 1945 and agreed that others shouldn't use history against it. I eulogised China for lifting half a billion people from the third world to the middle class in scarcely a generation; the biggest advance in human well-being of all time. And when MH370 disappeared into the Southern Indian Ocean, Australia didn't question the cost or the legal responsibility for the search; we swiftly despatched planes and ships to scour the seas earning the gratitude of the Chinese whose citizens were the bulk of those lost.

When the WikiLeaks revelations began, I called the US President to assure him of the importance of American intelligence gathering and sharing and to let him know that, far from being embarrassed, Australia fully supported it continuing. When I went to Washington in July 2014, I told him that I wasn't coming to ask for something or to complain about something but to offer Australian support-in-strength for the then incipient campaign against the ISIS caliphate in Syria and Iraq. This reportedly led President Obama subsequently to observe that "the world needs more Tony Abbotts!"

Very early on in Operation Sovereign Borders, a senior official warned that closing down the people smuggling trade and the hundreds of deaths at sea that it had caused could lead to a rupture with Indonesia. This didn't happen, in part, I suspect, because a fortnight into my prime ministership, I'd flown to Jakarta to tell the Indonesians exactly what we were minded to do, including turn-backs. After WikiLeaks about alleged Australian spying, Indonesian police cooperation against people smuggling was indeed briefly scaled back but this didn't derail our campaign against people smuggling thanks to the depth of our pre-existing cooperation plus the vigour of our own interception and turn-around operations at sea.

"Say what you mean and do what you say" was the rule that the Abbott government attempted to live by. Where we were indeed able to "do what we said" – because the Senate's permission was not required – the Abbott government was pretty successful. The boats were stopped within just three months and the three big free trade deals that had been languishing for a decade were finalised within 13 months. Internationally at least, the two years of the Abbott government were a bit of a "purple patch" for Australia: we led the MH370 search; we led the global fury at the MH17 atrocity and channelled it against Russian aggression; after America, we were the biggest contributor to the campaign against the Islamist death cult in the Middle East; and our border protection policies, much tut-tutted about by do-gooders, came to be envied and even emulated by some countries in Europe.

The challenge for all Australian governments is to be as effective as we can be in contributing to a better world; and that means maximising our capacity to influence events. Obviously, Australia is part of a number of international organisations: the G20, Asia Pacific Economic Cooperation, the East Asian Summit, and the Commonwealth as well as the United Nations. These are useful forums for discussion but don't normally make things happen.

The most important group Australia belongs to is probably the least formal and the most rarely discussed: the "five eyes" intelligence partnership with the United States, Britain, Canada and New Zealand. This involves regular high level officials' discussions, frequent personnel exchanges and almost total sharing of intelligence material. In part, a continuation of World War Two arrangements; in part, an obvious counter to Cold War threats; and in part, the natural solidarity between like-minded countries that speak the same language; on security matters, the "five eyes" partners generally think and act as one, inevitably under American leadership. In Australia's case, the "five eyes" arrangements are reinforced by the annual AUSMIN and AUKMIN talks between Australian-and-US and Australian-and-UK foreign and defence ministers and senior officials.

An Australian prime minister should be able to take for granted a close, cordial and cooperative relationship with the US president, and with the British, Canadian and New Zealand prime ministers. In my time, that was certainly the case, despite my political differences with Barack Obama over climate change. The challenge is to try to ensure that on as many issues as possible, the countries with the most instinctive and deep-seated solidarity, are striving to bring about change for the better. That means as much official interaction as possible to discuss issues of common concern.

With my enthusiastic support, Prime Minister David Cameron was keen to organise a "four friends" summit – which eventually happened, albeit very informally, on the fringes of the G20 in Brisbane in late 2014. I was keen to broaden this to a "five eyes" summit but, alas, this never went beyond talk. It was always my hope to try to extend strategic intimacy from the "five eyes" to Japan, Singapore, India and Israel as well, given those countries' histories, interests, networks and intuitions. Thanks to the good work of recent Australian governments, as well as frequent leaders' meetings, there are now semi-annual foreign and defence ministers' meetings between us and, respectively, Japan, Singapore and India.

It's easy to disparage "talk-fests" and it's always a wasted opportunity when the meetings of close partners result in "pious declarations" rather than practical measures to meet common challenges. Still, these gatherings are critically important because they force decision makers in different countries to familiarise themselves with their partners' words, deeds and ways of thinking. Within reason, the more bi-lateral and pluri-lateral dialogues that we can institutionalise, the better for our standing and influence in the wider world.

To maintain them, however, we need to be ready to commit our attention, our resources, and our armed forces in ways that engage our partners and address their issues lest the arranging of meetings with Australia drop down their list of priorities. Meetings with Australia should never turn out to be just "boxes ticked" or pointless wastes of time. They have to make a difference.

Menzies had no doubt that it was in Britain's interests, as well as in Australia's, for Australia to be fully engaged in the direction of the Empire's war effort. He thought that we brought insights and understandings to the war's strategic direction that leaders in London might lack. He was sure that the ships, planes and men we contributed to the empire's global struggle gave us the moral standing to sit in the War Cabinet. It's hard to fault his thinking or to doubt its contemporary relevance albeit not just with the United Kingdom.

Consider the biggest geo-strategic blunder of modern times, the disbanding of the Iraqi army and the Iraqi civil service after the successful 2003 invasion. It meant a half million unemployed men with guns and a country that no one knew how to run. Imagine how much better the next few years might have turned out if American decision-makers had taken Australian and British concerns more seriously.

Managing the rise of China, dealing with Russian aggression in Eastern Europe and fostering reform within Islam are challenges of the highest order. I have deep respect for the collective wisdom of the US defence and foreign policy establishment but so many decisions turn on the instincts of leaders. This is where two or three heads may turn out to be rather better than just one.

7
WHAT THE BRITISH ARE DOING IN THIS WAR

Georgina Downer

When Sir Robert Menzies delivered his broadcast on 6 February 1942, he warned of the "acute danger" Australia faced. The grim tragedy of Pearl Harbour had been followed by Japan's assault on Malaya, Thailand and Singapore. Days after Menzies' broadcast, my grandfather fought in vain in Singapore against the Japanese and waited out the rest of the war in the Changi POW camp. Australian territory did not avoid attack, with the Japanese bombing Darwin and, not long after, attacking Sydney.

Danger was eventually averted with defeat of Germany and Japan by a coalition of Western liberal democracies including the United States, Britain – whom Menzies' praised for "having the courage to go to war and risk everything for a just cause" – and, of course, Australia.

Menzies' record peacetime term as prime minister began after the end of the Second World War and since that time Australia has not faced another direct attack on our territory from a foreign power. Our enjoyment of 75 years' of peacetime owes much to Menzies and the work of his Ministers for External Affairs, Spender, Casey and Hasluck. Australia has prospered under a liberal international order underpinned by respect for the sovereignty of states, democracy, free markets and free people, buttressed by the ANZUS Treaty and the role of the United States as the predominant world power.

Australia, as a staunch defender of this liberal international order and member of the community of liberal democracies, has navigated the post war years to build a prosperous and successful society. This didn't happen through pure dumb luck but because of the farsighted nation-building activities of the Menzies era which included courageously forging early ties with our Asian neighbours in those post-war years when the memories of Japanese brutality were most raw. It is because of this early work that we have lived in a period of prosperity and relative peace and stability.

You only need to open the newspaper these days to understand that this peaceful and prosperous existence that we take for granted is under threat. While the threat may not feel as clear and present as the danger described by Menzies in 1942, it is real, multifaceted and growing. The threat to Australia's peaceful and prosperous position in the liberal international order begins from within. This is what makes it all the more insidious.

Regardless of one's views of President Trump's unorthodox leadership style and often ham-fisted attempts to articulate his message, Trump has been clear-eyed in identifying the West's growing lack of belief in and commitment to our values. In Warsaw in July 2017, President Trump asked "whether the West has the will to survive?" He went on to say that "Our own fight for the West does not begin on the battlefield -- it begins with our minds, our wills, and our souls."

In modern Australia, the issue is no different. Unlike our forebears who died to uphold our freedoms and way of life in the Second World War, modern-day Australia is becoming a society overcome with timidity when it comes to defending democracy, the rule of law, equality and respect for individual rights and freedoms.

Today, polarising voices tell us that speech which hurts feelings or makes people feel unsafe should be prohibited; others claim that our British history is shameful and we should distance ourselves from its monuments and legacies. Government – not the people

– knows best, we are told. The rule of one system of Australian law for all Australians is also challenged in our modern age; some would prefer the introduction of pluralist legal systems; others seek to rewrite the Constitution to accommodate separate rights for indigenous and non-indigenous Australians.

If we don't win the internal battle for hearts and minds and preserve our fundamental freedoms and the rule of law in Australia, we will be ill-equipped to confront the increasingly assertive revisionist nations who challenge our liberal international order.

The insidious rise of the self-doubting West also threatens the international institutions which underpin the liberal international order. Multilateral fora like the United Nations are increasingly unwieldy and impotent, while at the same time dominated by nations who don't share our respect for democracy and human rights. The world can ill-afford a multipolar world where illiberal authoritarian regimes like China and Russia are calling the shots in increasingly illiberal multilateral fora like the United Nations.

Other pan-national bodies such as the European Union suffer from Byzantine bureaucratic growth and overreach. Infringements on the Westphalian model of state sovereignty – a model which at its heart is democratic with each citizen connected to a local government rather than a distant elite – have been met with Brexit.

Erosion of belief in our Western values may be linked to the failure of globalist institutions and power. Moves towards global government, as is the case with the European Union, have led to anti-immigrant sentiments as citizens feel their governments have lost control of their borders. While the free and open markets in developed countries have delivered global prosperity, some in the West feel they have missed out on the spoils of globalisation and consider themselves part of a growing class of losers of globalisation.

Aggressive and authoritarian nations such as China and Russia, and intolerant and totalitarian movements like Islamic State take advantage of the cracks emerging in the West's liberal beliefs and institutions to fulfil their own revisionist ambitions.

China, with its authoritarian one-party state and expansionist tendencies, presents a threat to the rules-based order under which we have prospered. Australia has of course benefited from the rise of China's economy. Its demand for our natural resources and growing investment in our economy has provided us with many years of prosperity and hopefully this will continue in the years to come.

At the same time however, China has been modernising its military, growing its capacity to project its power beyond its territorial waters and exercising 'soft' power in developing nations in Asia and Africa. Last year, China launched its first home-made aircraft carrier to give it blue water capability. None of this should come as a surprise – with a growing economy and history of great power status, China wants a military might to match its economic power and prestige.

But the question remains: what is China doing with this new found status?

With its growing confidence in its economic and military might, China has adopted an increasingly aggressive position on its territorial disputes, flouting international laws and rules governing the settlement of these disputes. China's activities in the South China are the most egregious. China has systematically built islands, including airstrips and military installations, in the contested waters to buttress its claims to almost 90 per cent of the South China Sea. An international tribunal ruled in 2016 that China's claims in the waters near the Philippines were baseless. China refused to accept this decision. More recently, China's threats to take military action against Vietnamese bases in the South China Sea, led Vietnam to abandon drilling in contested waters.

China's aggressive and threatening behaviour in the South China Sea and refusal to accept a rules-based order are deeply troubling. Sixty per cent of Australia' trade flows through these waters. If China took control of the South China Sea it could dictate which vessels travel through the waters, interrupting freedom of navigation through these vital sea lanes. This then becomes a serious issue for Australia's future prosperity.

But on a broader level, with Southeast Asian nations increasingly capitulating to China's bully-boy tactics, if we are not careful the balance in the Indo-Pacific will shift towards Chinese dominance. China's One Belt One Road initiative is part of this broader regional push. A region where it's China calling the shots, without the Western constraints of democracy and the rule of law and with little regard to global rules and norms, is likely to be fraught with risks and flash points. Have no doubt, China's global leadership would not be benign.

For Australia we need the United States to refocus on the Indo-Pacific. We must fight against continued US disengagement from our region and the world. The Obama Administration, which was strong on rhetoric but weak on action to defend our values, rejected the legacy of decades of US global leadership and oversaw eight years of American decline. Throughout that time China took advantage of the absence of US leadership in the Indo-Pacific, in the South and East China Sea and in multilateral fora like the East Asia Summit. North Korea used the "strategic patience" of the Obama Administration to fast-track its development of nuclear warheads and ballistic missiles to become the single biggest threat to regional peace and security we have seen in a generation.

Revisionist states like Russia and Iran have also taken advantage of the West's flagging self-belief and US retrenchment. Russia used the Obama Administration's disengagement from global leadership to retake former Soviet territories such as Crimea in

Ukraine and prop up murderous regimes like that of Bashar al-Assad in Syria.

Increasingly, Russia and China have moved beyond territorial expansionism to begin to influence and subvert our own democratic and free societies. In the case of China, we've seen pressure put on Chinese diaspora here in Australia to toe the Communist Party line including in our universities, and the buying up of Chinese-language media to influence freedom of the press and speech in Australia. Russia has used advances in cyber technology and warfare to attempt to subvert democratic elections in the United States and France.

In our near neighbourhood, the threat of Islamist terrorism is taking root once again in Southeast Asia, particularly in the southern Philippines, but also in Islamic countries such as Malaysia and Indonesia. We need to support the efforts of our neighbours to fight off this scourge, not just because it represents a security risk to ourselves and our neighbours, but because of the totalitarian jihadist's threat to Western civilisation's values of democracy, the rule of law and individual freedoms. We mustn't adopt the appeasement policies of leaders like John Curtin who believed it was the actions of democratic nations that created fascism in our enemies and that "No war ... should be ... fought either to defend or to create political systems against other political systems."

Unlike our grandparents' generation, we are blessed to have never lived through a world war. The vast majority of families in Australia do not know the pain and agony of losing a loved one on the battlefield. We want to keep it that way. But our freedoms cannot be taken for granted. We are told we are at an inflection point in global history. The US-led liberal international order must prevail but this will take a lot more self-belief in the universality of our values, and a much stronger commitment to defend these values. While the neoconservative agenda of democracy promotion abroad may be out of favour, it is worth reflecting that liberal democracies do not go to war with each other. Economic interdependencies are important, but not definitive of future clashes. The evidence is that authoritarian states do not become truly advanced societies unless they move in a liberal democratic direction. The battle for the hearts and minds of freedom starts at home, but we should not give up that battle abroad.

8
Hatred as an Instrument of War Policy

Concetta Fierravanti-Wells

Written in April 1942, this essay was set at the height of the war and anti-Japanese propaganda. The atrocities of the war were foremost. Families lost their loved ones. The enemy was hated.

Menzies' concerns were that the propaganda was proceeding on the no doubt honestly held belief that a spirit of hatred amongst our own people is a proper instrument of war.

He asked himself the question: Are Australians so lacking in the true spirit of citizenship that they need to be artificially filled with the spirit of hatred?

Seventy-five years on it is a question that still holds true. Today's war is much more insidious with atrocities abounding. Terrorism and the hatred it engenders, can strike at the very heart of our society, literally as you walk down the street. This makes instilling fear and engendering hatred just as easy as in 1942.

Menzies oversaw one of the biggest shifts in Australian population growth through his migration policies. This included my father who came to Australia in 1953 and my mother in 1959.

Our post-war migration included migrants from countries we had fought against. Just as Australians put aside their hatred, they too expected migrants to leave their own hatred behind. Menzies' enlightened approach had the potential to go wrong, but it didn't. He set about creating a framework of nation building and laid the foundation of a solidly cohesive society.

As the daughter of migrants myself, I understand the hard work and sacrifices that motivated millions of people to come to Australia to build a better life for themselves and their children. This common thread was the glue that bound together people of different cultures, heritages, languages and religions. Hatred was set aside to re-build our nation and as Menzies had written, peace did close the door on war and opened the door to better things.

Today, we have grown to a population of 25 million people with about half of us born overseas or with at least one parent born overseas. Over a quarter of us speak a language other than English at home.

We respect diversity but we look, as former Prime Minister Howard said, at the things that unite us rather than the things that divide us.

But as Australia has journeyed towards this uniquely Australian multicultural society, there have been difficult moments.

With each wave of migration, communities faced challenges as they settled, accepted and in turn, became accepted. There were unfounded suspicions and resentment among established populations as each community made their journey of integration into Australian society. Their habits, lifestyles and food were different. They were called wogs and dagos.

But with time, Australians did not, as Menzies urged, let hatred overcome their judgement.

As the children of migrants went to schools and as migrants worked in the factories and worshipped together, barriers fell, experiences were shared; life's challenges became common amongst different groups and the rich tapestry that is today contemporary mainstream Australia began to be forged.

We have seen this pattern since the early days of European settlement, when Chinese, Irish and Germans were targeted. From the post-war migration boom, it was the Italians and Greeks, followed by Vietnamese and Lebanese in the 1970s, and more recently, Muslim groups.

In that journey, each came to what I term, their "cross-roads" moment. That moment when the community says: we are part of Australia; we have come here; we have left our homes; our children were born here; we have made sacrifices to get here; they cannot be in vain; and we cannot let our positive contribution to Australia be judged by the actions of a few rotten apples in our community.

And so, today it is the Muslim communities that are facing their "cross-roads" moment, complicated by the rise of fundamentalist Islamic terrorism and its impact across the world.

The 2016 Census indicates we remain a religiously diverse nation, with Christianity the most common religion (52%) and Islam (2.6%) and Buddhism (2.4%) the next most common religions. There are now about 620,000 Muslims in Australia, up from 2.2% in the 2011 Census. A majority of the communities are Australian born and aged less than 30 years.

Though relatively small in number, the Muslim communities are being viewed with suspicion and called on to publicly reaffirm their commitment to Australia.

Of course all Australians have a responsibility to Australia – it comes as the corollary to the rights we enjoy and the responsibilities we have as citizens, whether by birth or by choice. It is a critical part of maintaining our social cohesion.

But like so many communities before them, the Muslim communities need to make sure the positive narrative of their contribution over the centuries is not overshadowed by the negative publicity generated by the actions of a few.

In 2015, as Parliamentary Secretary to the Attorney General and to the Minister for Social Services and recognising the need for greater community engagement in countering violent extremism, I wrote to 160 Muslim organisations and had the opportunity to meet with many of them across Australia.

Regrettably, whilst we have seen young people of different backgrounds preyed upon by those bent on radicalising them, the most affected cohort have been some young Muslim Australians.

We need to deal with the reasons for the disengagement of these young Muslim Australians – the why. As many community leaders around Australia told me, if their young people had jobs, they wouldn't be vulnerable, nor have the inclination, or time to be radicalised. But there are prejudices.

In 2016, whilst at a function, I spoke to a group of business people. I asked them: if you had to hire someone and you had three CVs, all with equal qualifications, from Fred, Mario or Mohammed, who would you employ? No one spoke. The looks on their faces answered my question.

To meet these difficult challenges, we need to understand the social, cultural and religious complexities of the problem. To me, this is the essence of what Menzies was talking about. Rather than fostering hatred, deal with the issues head on.

To resolve the challenge of "radicalisation", it means working with communities at risk to ensure they not only "own" the problem but support them to "own" the solution. With hindsight, I do not believe that we have done so effectively in the past, but we very much need to do so in future.

It is not a vague or general responsibility but one that now falls on parents, community leaders, friends and families who are close to someone who is disillusioned with their life or misguidedly find an attraction to Daesh or ISIS. These people are the front line – the first to see changes in a person who is becoming radicalised and stop that young person before he or she goes too far down the wrong path.

I appreciate from my many consultations across the spectrum of the Muslim communities, many are fearful because they are being targeted by some Australians who prefer to hate, rather than understand that the bad deeds are being done by a few. They can face prejudice, especially women who have often borne the brunt of abuse because of their attire.

As Liberals, we believe in the inalienable rights and freedoms of all people, including freedom to practise their religion and beliefs without intimidation or interference, so long as those practices are within Australian law.

Today, banning the burqa has crystallised this fear and suspicion that some have for Muslim Australians. At a time of heightened security, we need to balance freedom and security and ensuring laws relating to identification are properly observed.

In my extensive community activities over the past 35 years, I have occasionally seen women wearing a burqa or a niqab, but mostly they wear a hijab, chador or dupatta where the face is fully seen. I have spoken with women and asked: Does the Quran obligate you to cover your face? The most common answer is: "No, it doesn't, it's my choice and what I feel best expresses my customs and beliefs." The Quran speaks about modesty of dress; it does not proscribe a dress code.

Against this, the burqa has however come to be associated with oppression. Recent scenes from areas liberated from Daesh domination show women burning the burqas they were forced to wear and men shaving off beards.

This comes at a time when Muslim communities are increasingly being called upon to stand up for Australian values, not just in words but in actions.

In any war, intelligence is vitally important. Most of the recent terrorist attempts have been foiled following intelligence from the community. In alerting authorities they have put their duty to Australia, its laws and values ahead of competing concerns for family or friends whose actions sought to harm Australians.

Recent events are a sober reminder of why the Australian Government is committed not only to fighting terrorism and extremism, but needs to work with communities at risk to face these challenges. No matter how effective we seek to make our law enforcement structures, without intelligence and without co-operation from these communities, our fight is a much harder one.

Menzies conclusions resonate seventy-five years on: "This does not mean that we are to be soft or hesitant or anything other than determined and ruthless in our search for victory. It does not mean that in some dreamy or philosophic fashion we are to forget that the salvation of mankind requires that this generation of ours should be ready to go through hell to defeat it devils. But it does mean that we should refuse to take the honest and natural and passing passions of the human heart and degrade them into sinister and bitter policy."

Menzies' migration legacy lives on. We have become one of the most culturally diverse yet socially cohesive nations on earth. It is vitally important that the great legacy of our migration history not be blemished by the hatred of a few.

9
SCRAP IRON FOR JAPAN

Andrew Bragg

Menzies' home truth to Australians during our battle for survival in World War II was: Australia will either trade or die.

The principle is timeless. We must permanently nourish the argument that an open, outward looking, competitive economy delivers opportunity for all Australians.

Menzies noted on face value, not every single international transaction would appear immediately desirable, but exports were essential for prosperity.

He said in the broadcast: "the whole economy of this country has rested upon our great exports, and upon the willingness of foreign countries to buy them."

Menzies took the opportunity to defend accusations his 1939-1941 government provided scrap iron to Japan which was subsequently used in ammunition against Australian soldiers.

His simple response was Australia provided Japan an enormous amount of wool and wheat over the same period and there is no difference between feeding, clothing and arming soldiers and being selective about exports would only lead to ruin.

A timeless principle

To demonstrate the timelessness of the principle, a similar discussion was held in the mid 1980s on the desirability of uranium trade: Australia is now the world's third largest exporter of uranium.

Yet this was not assured until the Hawke government won the argument against internal constituents who wanted to lock uranium up and leave it in the ground forever.

Thirty years on, any reasonable person would agree failing to utilise the world's biggest deposit of uranium would be scandalous. The almost 5,000 jobs in the Australian uranium industry are found in very remote parts where employment opportunities can be few and far between.

The principles equally apply henceforth to energy policy. We must not forget Australia is an energy superpower.

All policy settings applying to energy and resources such as coal and gas must be evaluated through the prism of trade and competitiveness.

This does not mean we have an excuse to avoid climate change commitments Australia makes through the United Nations and other bodies.

But it does mean we cannot afford to put ideology before science when we consider the policy settings applying to renewable energy, gas exploration and any other market intrusion such as a carbon tax. As we consider the future of onshore gas exploration, much of which is locked up, we ought to remember the uranium debate was nearly lost.

No person, and certainly no country, can be granted great endowments and decide not to use them because last year's profits or efforts can be relied upon.

It is not a sustainable model. Opportunities are finite and the culture of the lucky country will not do.

We must turn the endowments into opportunities. We must make the opportunities count.

The truth is, we in Australia, with a large landmass with a small population, now on the doorstep of Asia's booming middle class, are born to look outwards.

The mere fact trade opens opportunities and improves lives should be ingrained by the millions of individual experiences of typical Australians.

It was in my family. For instance, my grandfather James from Stawell in Victoria, fought the Japanese in New Guinea in the 1940s but would only purchase Mitsubishi cars from the 1980s. He did so because they provided the best station wagon to suit his fishing gear.

We cannot survive without open trade. Yet, this fact will be contested forever.

Two lessons

Menzies' framework attains timelessness by doing two things for us today:

1. Reasserting the value of trade to Australia and the ever-present opportunities of our geography
2. Calling out protectionism in all its guises

The opportunity of trade

Australians exploiting trade opportunities dates to Macarthur and his wool bales at the beginning of the 19th century. Trade is in our DNA.

We should remember the key statistics. Australia did not become the 12th largest economy on earth with just the 50th largest population by accident. Exports account for 40 per cent of our gross domestic product and one in five jobs is directly linked to export trade.

The development of export industries such as iron ore, gas, gold and coal was the result of vision, tenacity and opening frontiers in domestic development, such as Lang Hancock, Peter Wright and Sir Richard Court in Western Australia, but also through opening international trade opportunities.

Menzies' capacity to see the benefit of trade with the most brutal of enemies during World War II was truly remarkable. He followed up with the 1957 Australia Japan Commerce Agreement which opened iron ore exports to Japan.

But we have not continued to grow for 27 years without being linked to the world. In most export markets, our customers have other options and we do not enjoy a monopoly.

Recent prosperity has rested upon a combination of industry and political leadership to develop the country, along with a reform dividend from decades past which has boosted our national competitiveness.

By 2030, three billion people will be in the Asian middle class to our north. That's roughly a billion in India, China and South East Asia.

Our largest trading partners are already in North Asia and the emergence of India, Indonesia and South East Asia will only provide more opportunities to export products and services.

Services are just 17 per cent of our exports yet represent 70 per cent of our gross domestic product. As the middle classes of Asia swell, they will increasingly demand services – think accounting, legal, architecture, education, tourism, finance and professional services.

With Australia's population unlikely to exceed 40 million in coming decades, we must do all we can to plug into the extraordinary growth of the Asian middle class.

With this at stake, realism not dogma must govern our mindset.

Protectionist messages are commonplace in Trump's America

and omnipresent in the European Union, which has failed to be a paragon of free trade beyond its own borders.

Australia cannot afford to follow the leader on talk or actions which reflect protectionism. This would be the worst time to succumb to protectionism.

The trouble is, we often suffer collective amnesia on sometimes dry policy areas like trade and look to ideas we dismissed just a generation ago.

On the domestic side of the coin, we see suggestions of reimposing Australian tariffs or local content requirements floated on a regular basis.

The highly protected, rigid and uncompetitive "Australian settlement" featured high tariffs, subsidies, centralised wage fixing and Canberra-controlled banking arrangements. It was established in the years following federation in 1901 and became an article of faith for all political parties.

The Settlement was finally despatched to the dustbin in the 1980s and 1990s after decades of work initially from Bill Carmichael, Bert Kelly and later Bob Hawke, Paul Keating, and John Howard.

Australia's economy responded with 27 years of growth (so far) after being opened to the world.

One risk of Trump's new nationalism (America First) is we feel compelled to exhume some of these discredited policy settings.

It provides an opportunity to pursue competitiveness at all costs. Long may we remember the great lesson of the "Australian Settlement": it did not work.

We should not seek rinky-dink solutions such as tariffs, prescriptive local content requirements, new taxes or indiscriminate, poorly constructed cuts to immigration.

The Productivity Commission estimate a trade war which adopts a cascading "America First" approach would cost Australia 100,000 jobs and reduce $1,500 from average incomes.

If it was impossible to coset Australia away from 1901 to 1980, it would be futile to try it in an age of increasing capital mobility, technology and rapid communication.

As President Trump looks to renegotiate the highly successful North American Trade Agreement and pull back on international collaboration, we should thrust forward to pursue all available trade agreements.

If we keep all our irons in the fire, we will maximise our chances of getting deals done. Bilateral, multilateral or plurilateral should all be in the mix.

All irons in the fire should be our credo rather than Australia First.

Regional agreements such as the Trans Pacific Partnership and the Regional Comprehensive Economic Partnership bear the makings of an Asian region free trade zone.

As it is likely to take decades to assemble the regional architecture, a program for bilateral agreements with all major Asian economies should be completed by 2025.

The trouble with trade agreements is once they are inked by the Trade Minister, there is a perception it is the end of the work. The truth is that a trade agreement is just the beginning.

Two outcomes must be top of mind for Australian trade policy development in the coming decades.

One: a program for implementation of trade commitments should be rolled out to every industry and regulator to reflect a trade agreement is the "end of the beginning" of an export, not the "beginning of the end".

Two: every trade agreement must have a schedule for review and continuous improvement above and beyond conventional trade agreement mechanisms such as "most favoured nation" clauses.

Spotting protectionism

For an export reliant nation like Australia, protectionism is worse than cancer.

Yet protectionism is never far away. It is harder to spot than it was in Menzies' day.

In Menzies day, the Opposition and a bunch of industries shamefully opposed his 1957 commerce agreement purely for race and economic reasons.

Today the protectionists are too embarrassed to make such discredited arguments. Instead they oppose trade agreements for legalistic reasons – always cloaked in an emotive shell.

Protectionism remains an agenda for isolationism.

The protectionists favourite red herring is Investor State Dispute Settlement (ISDS) – clause in trade agreements which is claimed to threaten the "sovereignty" of the state.

It is a little-known clause but it is being used to stop trade deals.

At a functional level, ISDS is a legal mechanism for resolving cross border investment disputes between business and nations. It allows a business which is doing business abroad to protect their property rights in the event a host state damages their investment.

Typically, disputes are addressed through tribunals established by the World Bank or Hague Convention.

ISDS reinforces the rule of law and strengthens investment into developing countries as Asian Development Bank studies have shown.

No nation has ever lost an ISDS case which has impinged a social, health or environmental law.

Australian companies are starting to make the most of the opportunities of the Asian middle class by investing in the region.

In South East Asia, the legal systems are less certain and Australian companies have used ISDS to resolve investment disputes.

Most of the discussion in Australia's media over the past decade on ISDS has focused on a negative idea that "foreign companies shouldn't sue governments". It may sound good but it smacks of provincialism and ignores key democratic principles.

This very unscientific argument neglects to remember we accept in a democracy that no person, lawmaker or government is above the law and that we can test laws in the courts.

Australia waited almost a decade for trade deals with China and Japan because ISDS had caused such consternation in the Rudd-Gillard government of 2007-13.

Deals were only done with Korea, then Japan and China after ISDS was put back on the table by former Trade Minister Andrew Robb in 2014.

The often-cited ISDS case is Philip Morris' action against the Australian Government on plain packaging cigarettes.

This case is now held out as a reason to never again agree to ISDS clauses or worse, to reopen every single trade agreement Australia has struck and renegotiate it to remove ISDS.

Talk about flagging your strategy to your competitors before commencing negotiations!

The fly in the ointment on cigarettes is Australia won the Philip Morris case. As did Uruguay in a similar case brought under an ISDS clause.

With entire union-driven protest movements now established to fight ISDS, we must ask why? It must be the latest iteration of the protectionists' tools.

Arguing against ISDS is akin to arguing directly against trade. We must not succumb to the simplicity of the arguments and look behind to see it for what it is: protectionism and isolationism.

The motives for the isolation agenda amongst the union movement are clear. Unions want to keep what they have (provincial power and relevance). They believe Australia can swim against the tide. As a nation that relies on foreign capital and open export markets, it will not work.

Ultimately, the desire of most Australians is to get a job and deliver for their family. This will only be possible under policies which promote trade, investment, openness and regional engagement.

Whether we keep the gates open to trade and investment will heavily determine the ultimate length of Australia's world-beating run of economic growth.

10
THE CENSORSHIP

Peter Phelps

We all understand why section 18C is a problem. Government should not be in the business of telling people what they can or cannot say.

But there is an even more insidious form of censorship, one that threatens public debate more than the punitive efforts of the state: the self-censorship of the political pragmatist.

A significant problem with contemporary politics is the woeful level of discussion which passes for political communication amongst the political class. Even a casual observer, with little more than a rudimentary understanding of politics and society, is continually tempted to point out logical errors, bad analysis, false syllogisms and opinion-masquerading-as-fact.

Liberal backbenchers have pretty free reign to say what they like without violating any Party rules. But that is not what happens for most Members.

Most MPs use their opportunity to communicate, both inside and outside of Parliament, for little more than retail politics: "MP announces new roundabout funding", or "Here I am opening the local fete". The politics of the parish pump and the pork barrel is how both major parties tell their MPs to use their time.

Why is this so? Some MPs are just bad at arguing their case in any forum, because they have no idea what the Party stands for, and have little or no background in political thought. They are the proverbial 'person off the street' so beloved by our political mythologisers. For them, the "We Believe" statement is as unimportant to their political lives as a tablet of Babylonian cuneiform.

If these MPs were ever to try to argue an ideological case they would likely be bested by the high-sounding and falsely-cogent positions of practised Leftists. So the advice is this: "don't say anything" or "silence never got anyone into trouble" or "keep focussed on local issues".

These know-nothing MPs are a blight. The only outcome they seek is personal acclaim, and maybe a plaque with their name upon it, via the channelling of government largesse into their seats. They could probably be MPs from any other party and no-one could tell the difference.

Other MPs believe that to take up the cudgels of ideology is a poor use of their finite and precious time. They acutely feel that anything they say must be anodyne, perky and uplifting, or they will offend somebody who votes in their electorate. Heaven forbid that any MP should be anything more than a cipher for their constituents' unquenchable appetites!

They are told that they must win their seats. But when the question arises as to what they are wining those seats for: no response, except perhaps for the simple, negative agenda of 'keeping the other side out of power'. Their political life culminates in the presentation of a giant novelty cheque through an unending cycle of 'rubber chicken' dinners for service and community groups.

It is the politics of "blah, blah, blah", an Orwellian duck-speak which provides grist for the mill of local media; an ersatz meal which briefly fills the bellies but neither satisfies the cook, nor nourishes the diners.

But there is an especially low rung of Hell reserved for those MPs who should know better, but choose not to be better. Those who could, if they wanted to do so, engage in the war with the Left, yet decline to do so.

Cynical, preening careerists with an overwhelming fear that they may offend somebody; or that their words might appear in the newspapers 'out of context'; or that the Leader might be upset if they say anything out of the ordinary (which could possibly weaken their chances for promotion); or the Party Director will not make theirs a 'key seat' in the next election campaign because they departed from the daily-scripted, key-points fed out to them; or for any of a host of other reasons. All of which boil down to this: cowardice.

How can this happen? Our society is a product of our education. Across all spectrums of education we have come to accept an pedagogy which rewards passive compliance with received wisdom over inquiry and debate. Argument is unseemly, threatening or – in the modern parlance – 'triggering', and thus must be avoided at all cost.

Political warriors must start from a different premise: that we are engaged in a cultural fight with the Left of politics for the future of this nation and the Western world. People on our side may not yet realise that we are at war, but the Left certainly does.

So far they have conquered our schools and universities, our public services, the arts, and a substantial portion of our media. Our discourse is set by Left NGOs, supported by Left academics and artists appearing in Left media, with their aim being the extension of regulation and government – and hence more Left public servants.

Our traditional concepts of rights have been turned around, to instead become a grab-bag of 'feels' and Socialistic incursions into our true freedoms. What the Socialists could not gain by revolution, they now advance through a cultural Fabianism that seeks out the young and, in the main, stands unchecked by any political figures on the Right.

There is no better, or rather worse, example of this than contemporary phenomenon of social media. Social media is, in many ways, a replacement for the old 'town hall meetings' that were the staple of MPs in previous eras.

There was once a time where, if a political leader wanted to broadcast their message, they had to get out into the community. Far from the safe, scripted and homogenised theatre of today's political meetings, the local meeting in the School of Mechanics Hall, was a wild, rambunctious affair.

Anyone could turn up to hear your views on political topics, but you must expect hecklers too. The greats of Australian political debate all cut their teeth is just such an environment. It is where politicians were made and unmade, in an arena of ideas, wit, ridicule and presentation.

No Socialist ever went to a public meeting to hear a speech by Menzies and walked out as a Capitalist. But it is an unspoken – although seldom acknowledged – truth that there are few things more enjoyable to watch than a good fight. While such a view may be a generalisation for the community at large, it is especially true for the self-selecting politically-minded.

People may not wish to be involved directly in the fight, but there is an undeniable vicarious pleasure in watching your opponents get trounced in debate or humiliated through a magnificent put-down.

But these days, political figures are wrapped in cotton wool. They go to kindergartens for photo ops and complacent, compliant audiences. The message, if there even is one, is mashed into a gruel of sound-bites and focus-grouped phrases, repeated over and over again to 'get the message through'.

Yet this is an exercise in futility. There is a very important, but often ignored, modern phenomenon – the desire for 'authenticity' which modern consumers seek in more and more aspects of their daily lives.

Authentic apples have blemishes, not waxy perfection; authentic music is written by the performers, not the producers; authentic politicians talk from the heart, not the script.

Now, of course, all of this demand has opened up a whole new market for the supply of fake 'authenticity' – other political analysts have observed and discussed this phenomenon – which is just as eagerly consumed by apple-eating, music-loving voters. But that is beside the point.

The point is that the political effectiveness of scripted comments and behaviour is now rapidly diminishing. If you watch audiences listen to most political speeches, you can see even supportive audiences 'turn off'. Their heads are down, their phones are out.

The political impact fails miserably because the scripted message is so obviously forced, and people put up barriers at what they see as a poorly contrived attempt to connect with them.

Ending the self-censorship that we impose on ourselves allows us to avoid the tedium of conventionality. It also has the great advantage of being undeniably theatrical, and thus entertaining – perfect for an audience which demands to be entertained and has a multitude of options in various mediums from which to choose.

That does not mean that such performance is value-free or politically neutral. Indeed, the propaganda value of "the show" stretches back to Ancient Greece, and has been evident in modern times from the "Battleship Potemkin" or "Birth of the Nation" through to the music of Midnight Oil.

Our predecessor politicians were forced to hone their skills, their arguments, their witticisms, their theatricality on public stages and in halls with staunch allies, robust opponents, and outright troublemakers.

So too should the capable modern politician engage, fight, and ridicule on the modern public stage, without the dead hand of self-censorship strangling the vitality and authenticity of that debate.

11
THE NEW MINISTER TO WASHINGTON

Josh Frydenberg

In 1942, Prime Minister John Curtin thrust the then High Court Justice Sir Owen Dixon into an unanticipated and unaccustomed role in public life. Dixon was appointed Australia's Minister to the United States. The times called for much more than a capable diplomat or skilled politician who, in Menzies' words, simply had a "capacity for easy good fellowship". The times were grave and complex. They required, as Menzies would later remark in *The Forgotten People*, a person with "flexibility of mind, constructive capacity and marked judgement". As his country's representative, the Minister was required not only to be an exemplar of the highest standards, but to use his "penetrating eye and clear understanding" to communicate to the American government and its people the significance of Australia to the overall war effort. Dixon did an outstanding job.

Given the enormity of the challenge, Menzies knew that his mentor Sir Owen Dixon was equal to the task. Dixon was the best of his generation. He combined "shining integrity, academic and legal pre-eminence and administrative gifts of a high order" and beyond that he was to Menzies "a most distinguished representative of the best Australian culture and civilisation".

Menzies' insight more than 70 years ago into the key characteristics required to deal with matters impacting on Australia's future are still true today. There may not be the prospect of troops massing at our border or an eminent threat of totalitarianism on the march, but we do face significant challenges which, if inadequately met, could undermine our way of life. We need people in public office, public service and public life who reflect the qualities Menzies so aptly described. At the end of the day, it's about integrity, capacity, judgement and vision.

Integrity requires principles and values that are constant and the ability to determine right from wrong. Just as no political party has a monopoly on compassion, there are people of integrity who can be found on both sides of the political divide. Much more than by what someone says, their integrity is best measured by what they actually do. The test in acutely challenging times is the fundamental distinction between doing something that is simply popular and doing what is right – and this is the test. A fortnightly poll is of itself neither necessary nor sufficient to prescribe a leader's course of action, nor should it of itself impact on the nature of advice from the public service. Without integrity, there can be no trust. Without trust, the political compact in our democracy between the public and their leaders is undermined.

Integrity is necessary, but our leaders need more. They need to be capable. As Dixon's appointment demonstrated, what qualified him for office was the scope of his ability and the nature of his personal attributes, not the direct experience he may have acquired in a particular line of endeavour. Today, the challenges of public policy are so fast moving that adaptability and lateral thinking are key. One of the consequences of the digital revolution is that the traditional models of social and economic interaction are being disrupted. The flow, interpretation and understanding of data is turning the accepted wisdoms of banking, communications, logistics, retail and energy to name but a few areas on their head. This requires minds that engage openly and responsibly. We should include more people in the parliament, bureaucracy and public life who come to the table with the experience of having taken decisions with consequences and who understand that the capacity to be objectively critical of prior decisions, including their own, is a virtue. This could be experience gained in business, the professions or social, political, or civic enterprise. But above all it is people who have taken responsibility for their own decisions and the decisions of others. One should never underestimate the importance of wisdom borne of experience. History demonstrates this.

We also need a number of senior public servants who come to their role with previous meaningful exposure to non-government work. As both a Minister and ministerial adviser, I found the Commonwealth public service to be highly professional, capable and committed to serving faithfully the government of the day. For this, we should be grateful. Arguably, at times though, the public service is too cautious and conservative in its propagation of ideas, being content to make the case for incremental change or slight variants of the status quo. There are circumstances that justify examining a topic or a problem with a clean sheet of paper. This requires bravery, a certain boldness and an innovative approach. People who come to the public service with external experience may not just bring a capacity, but also a confidence to look at challenging issues in unconventional and often less obvious ways.

A third quality which is fundamental to sound leadership in public office is judgement, an elusive quality which is hard to define, but is obvious when it's absent. Judgement is all about understanding the environment in which one operates, the prospect of success, the consequences of failure and the people with whom you interact and ultimately need to take with you. Judgement requires both a short and longer term view. This is a real challenge in today's world where redundancy in methods and techniques, and outcomes occur much more rapidly than before. Decision points require judgment calls as to the shape of the future. Illustrations of this relate to the choices that need to be made around infrastructure roll outs, such as the NBN or the nature of new-build energy generation networks. Equally, but on a different intellectual, philosophical and practical plane is the question of how Australia positions itself in the region and indeed the world. This requires a sophisticated judgement. Dealing with the moving sands of diplomacy, economic growth and consequent inter-state rivalries, requires the best judgement because it has the most serious consequence. While we need to remain pragmatic, our strategic decision-making matrix must always reflect our fundamental values and who we are.

A final quality required in public life is often said to be a vision. A sense of inspiring a community with a direction in which to go. It's a short word with a big meaning and often invoked as an outcome in itself. This is a misuse of the term. The implementation of a false vision is folly and can be disastrous. The most extreme of this was Hitler's Third Reich. In many senses, the sharing of a vision should be a precondition to involvement in public life. We need leaders who combine integrity, capacity and judgement with a clear purpose, for this will define the parameters within which they operate and create a greater sense of certainty and trust. Not all visions need to be big, bold and brave or with immediate payoffs, but they do need to be consistent with community values and priorities. A good vision must address the legitimate interests of people with different needs, and overtime, it must be able to generate a broad consensus that its implementation will move the nation in the right direction. Ultimately, the reason why vision is so important is because it provides an intellectually satisfactory framework for decision-making at all stages along the route.

For a Liberal, the fundamental leadership framework puts at its core the freedom of the individual and their enterprise. It seeks to create a society which protects its weak and affords dignity for those who cannot provide for themselves. This is the Liberal way. It enshrines equality of opportunity and generally disdains the supressing socialist notion of equality of outcomes. The Liberal view of a virtuous state stands in stark contrast to the view that a better society is one which seeks as its primary objective to render all people equal through the operation and the instruments of the state. Today, we hear calls from the political left for democratic capitalism to be reshaped, be it by political leaders such as Jeremy Corbyn or academics like Thomas Piketty. Crises like the global financial crisis have been used by the political left as an occasion to over-expand the role the government. Here at home, under the apparent guise of creating a "fairer society", our political opponents are seeking to provide unearned redistribution of capital without recognising the implications for national wellbeing.

Though understandably everyone wants more, this can only be achieved by real economic growth, productivity gains and the maintenance of competition, not through virtue signalling and an assertion of moral superiority. The diminution of incentives to invest and grow, the imposition of barriers to an open economy and the creation of supersized unions with power over vertically integrated supply chains is antithetical to this objective. These policies in the context of a union and political culture which seeks to prescribe a moral basis to justify flagrant breaches of the law is an ominous threat to the prosperity, order and security of the nation as a whole. It is in this environment that is incumbent upon Liberals to constantly make the case that prosperity and a good, decent and fair society emerges from the application of its principles. Prosperity that Liberalism brings is both an economic and moral imperative.

As Australia's most success political leader, Sir Robert Menzies combined the science of good policymaking with the political art of persuasion and implementation. A key to his success was his understanding of the quality and nature of leadership. His prescription of what Owen Dixon brought to the role in Washington is a worthy guide for us today. Integrity, capacity, judgement and vision are the attributes we need in public life to drive forward as a nation.

12

OUR AMERICAN ALLIES

Andrew Shearer

In his Forgotten People broadcast, Robert Menzies looked to Australia's post-war future. It is easy to forget he was only able to do so because, just two weeks earlier, US and Australian naval forces had blocked a Japanese invasion force in the Coral Sea on its way to seize Port Moresby, on Australia's northern doorstep. Nonetheless, the climactic Battle of Midway was yet to come and Australia was still fighting for its life — or at least for its way of life — alongside a powerful but ambivalent new ally.

Seventy-five years later, we are still fighting together, against very different enemies. The Australia-US alliance remains, as Prime Minister Turnbull said in August 2017, the cornerstone of Australia's national security.

This was far from inevitable. America's defence of Australia during the Second World War was all about strategic geography, not sentiment. US South Pacific war supremo General Douglas MacArthur said as much when he told Prime Minister Curtin that America's sole interest in Australia was as a base from which to attack and defeat Japan. The United States showed little interest in maintaining a commitment to Australia in the years immediately following the war; belying subsequent mythology, even in 1943-44 Curtin continued to see Imperial defence as key to Australia's post-war security, and his successor Ben Chifley looked to a spent Britain to guarantee his nation's uncertain security in the early years of the Cold War. It took the shock of the Korean War to create the conditions for a formal alliance — and the vision, energy and diplomatic verve of Menzies' foreign minister, Sir Percy Spender, to seize the opportunity and engineer the ANZUS Treaty in 1951.

Today, the alliance still faces daunting threats and challenges.

North Korea already has the means to target Japan, South Korea and US military bases in the Western Pacific with conventional and nuclear-tipped ballistic missiles. It is rapidly developing intercontinental ballistic missiles capable of striking most of the United States (and Australia), as well as submarine-launched missiles. One of the North Korean leadership's key aims is to erode the confidence of America's allies — particularly South Korea and Japan — that Washington will risk defending them. The undermining of US alliances in the region — and ultimately even alliance "decoupling" — could have dire consequences, such as inducing Japan and South Korea to obtain their own nuclear weapons. Australia, along with fellow members of the United Nations Command in Korea, is technically still at war with North Korea and has substantial interests in Northeast Asian stability. In these circumstances it is difficult to take issue with the Prime Minister's assertion that Australia would be obliged to join the United States (and its other allies) in the event of a major conflict on the Korean Peninsula.

The disruption of a planned terrorist attack on an Australian airliner, along with attacks across Europe and the seizure of the southern Philippines town of Marawi by jihadis affiliated with Islamic State, highlight the continuing potency of Islamist extremism as a threat to Australia and its allies. The alliance — and the vital "Five Eyes" intelligence relationship — will remain at the core of Australia's efforts to deny safe haven to terror networks, disrupt their operations, and keep Australians as safe possible, at home and abroad (particularly in Southeast Asia). Australian aircraft and Army trainers have played an important part in US-led coalition operations against the Islamic State "caliphate" in Iraq and

Syria, and RAAF maritime surveillance aircraft are working with the US military in support of local security forces battling jihadis in the southern Philippines. Australian participation in robust counter-terrorism actions — in our region and beyond — is likely to remain an unfortunate reality for years, if not decades. So will the need to build the capacity and resilience of our Southeast Asian and South Pacific neighbours.

Acute as these threats are, it is China's growing power and assertiveness that is having the largest — and most deleterious — impact on Australia's strategic environment. For several decades Australia and its friends and allies have pursued policies based on engaging China, in the hope that as it rose that country would embrace open regional economic arrangements, the rule of law, and international principles such as freedom of navigation and the peaceful resolution of disputes.

Today, as President Xi Jinping strengthens his grip, those hopes look naive. China is using all of the instruments of its growing national power to carve out an old-fashioned sphere of interest in East Asia. It is deploying advanced missiles, aircraft and warships in increasing numbers (as well as sophisticated cyber, electronic warfare and space-based systems) to prevent the US Navy from projecting power into the Western Pacific – a mainstay of the region's stability and prosperity over the past 70 years. It has demolished pristine reefs, built islands and constructed extensive military facilities on disputed features in the South China Sea, positioning itself to assert effective military control over one of the world's most vital international waterways. At the same time it is using its rapidly expanding fleet of coastguard vessels (some larger than US guided-missile cruisers), along with economic coercion and bullying diplomacy, to bend regional countries to its will.

China is also buying domestic political influence to weaken the integrity of their institutions and undermine resistance to its agenda. These tactics are yielding some success in Southeast Asia, where a mix of intimidation and blandishments has seen a number of countries – most prominently Cambodia, the Philippines and Malaysia – start to "tilt" away from the United States and towards China. A series of cyber attacks, the "Dastyari affair" and subsequent media investigations (including a major expose on *Four Corners* of Chinese efforts to penetrate political parties, business, universities and Chinese-language media outlets) have revealed that Australia is far from immune from these efforts. Russia's efforts to interfere with the 2016 US election (and others across Europe) highlight the stakes.

Unlike Menzies when he gave his Forgotten People broadcast, we now know that in 1942 Australia did not confront the threat of invasion. But it did face the loss of its political independence had the Japanese invasion of Port Moresby succeeded. Cut off from the United States and its other allies, Australia would have had no choice but to accommodate itself to Japan's dictates.

Today's military threat is more remote (although China's growing arsenal of long-range conventional and nuclear missiles is eroding Australia's longstanding strategic depth). But the threats to what Menzies called "a fierce independence of spirit" – "the greatest element in a strong people" and "the only real freedom" – are real.

The cultural Left and other long-time opponents of Australia's alliance with the United States have been quick to seize on the Trump presidency as evidence of US decline and a pretext for Australia to distance itself from the United States and pursue a "more independent" foreign policy – code for watering down the alliance and accommodating China's regional security, political and economic preferences. Advocates of this policy rarely have the courage to specify what it means, but we should be clear-eyed about the consequences. Australia would break not only with the United States but with its most important regional partners, including Japan and India. It would turn a blind eye to worsening human rights abuses in China. It would acquiesce in China's militarisation of the South China Sea and bullying of Japan in the East China Sea. It would abandon Taiwan's 23 million democratic citizens (and Hong Kong) to their fate. It would effectively lose its ability to make its own sovereign decisions on foreign investment in Australia and on regional trade arrangements. And China would exercise a de facto veto over Australia's security cooperation with the United States and other likeminded democracies. We might be free of the risk of Chinese sanction or attack but would be left without a shred of self-respect.

Many of the same advocates argue that the only alternative is to risk being dragged into a major war by our alliance with the United States. This sells the pass, and in the process compromises both our values and our interests.

War in Asia is possible, but it isn't likely. China's strategy is based on achieving its strategic objectives without triggering a major conflict. Working closely with the United States – and with Japan, India, and other democratic regional partners – is the best way to reinforce the liberal regional order in the face of China's revisionism, bolster the confidence and resilience of wavering Southeast Asian nations, and push back against Chinese probing, wherever it occurs. As China's military and economic power grows, the best way to maintain an Asia Pacific balance of power that continues to favour freedom and openness will be for countries that share those values to work together – in the first instance to shape the region's continuing development and, in the last resort, to deter adventurism or aggression.

Australia will be tempted to mind its own business and let others do the heavy lifting, not least with an unpopular US president in office. As the late Michael Cook (former Director General of the

Office of National Assessments and Ambassador to the United States) recognised, however, far from undermining Australia's independence (as its critics claim), the alliance *strengthens* its ability to withstand any attempt China may make to use its economic leverage to influence sovereign economic, political and security choices. The Australian public seem to understand this too: polls show that they overwhelmingly recognise China's importance to Australian prosperity but also that a substantial majority consider the alliance important to Australia's national security, irrespective of US political leadership. President Trump's administration may not be the easiest or most predictable Australian governments have had to work with. But so far many of its foreign and security policies are consistent with Australia's interests, and some are an improvement on the previous president. Moreover, the alternatives – supine appeasement, armed neutrality (requiring at least a doubling of the current defence budget), or even acquiring an independent nuclear weapons capability – are ultimately much more costly.

What would Menzies have done?

It is certain that he would have navigated today's geopolitical flux by deploying all his pragmatism and guile in implacable pursuit of Australia's national interest, as he did during more than 18 years as prime minister. There seems little chance, however, that Menzies would have taken a backward step from the American alliance. Decades after his Forgotten People speech – at the height of the Vietnam War (a previous period in which Menzies noted it had become fashionable to criticise America and American policy) – he warned that regional economic and social progress would be held back unless aggression and subversion could be halted, and described the alliance as "the keystone of our Pacific structure". Typically, he was right then and he's still right now.

13
LEND-LEASE

Linda Reynolds

In May 1942 Robert Menzies commenced his weekly radio address with the observation "One of the many troubles, I was going to say of democracy, but perhaps I should say of ourselves as a people, is that we do not think enough and we take too many astonishing things for granted."

Then, as now, he could have been referring to a great many issues we take for granted in Australia. In this address he was referring to what Winston Churchill, the year before, had called "the most unsordid Act in recorded history". A big call for a Prime Minister fighting for his nation's very survival.

So what was this most astonishing and un-sordid of Acts? It was the Lend-Lease Act, a very short Statute passed by the American congress in March 1941 to "to promote the defence of the United States". The Act was instigated by President Roosevelt after a plea by Winston Churchill for the US, a neutral nation, to provide Great Britain with the tools to finish the war.

The Act conferred upon the President wide-ranging powers to authorise the selling, exchanging, leasing and lending of any such defence article "for the Government of any country whose defence the President deems vital to the defence of the United States". It also provided the President with post war powers to determine the terms and conditions upon which payment or re-payment was to be made – if they were to be repaid at all. Astonishing indeed. The congress of a neutral nation, not only giving their President wide ranging powers to provide billions of dollars of material support to other nations, but also with the power to determine if and how it would ever be repaid.

As astonishing as this un-sordid act was to both Churchill and Menzies, the motives, which effectively ended a decade of US neutrality, were complex, pragmatic and ultimately far-sighted. President Roosevelt knew Great Britain was running out of money to fund its war effort and when that happened, the US would have to enter the war to finish it themselves.

In this speech Menzies also observed that "too many of us are like the old man in the story who said, "Sometimes I sits and thinks, and sometimes I just sits". It was clear that as early as 1941-42 Roosevelt, Churchill and Menzies were not just sitting. They were thinking both about how to prosecute and win the war and also about how to reconstruct a post-war world and avoid the mistakes after World War One.

In 1941 Churchill provided both moral and economic reasons for US support. He said "the moment approaches when we shall no longer be able to pay cash for shipping and other supplies … if at the height of this struggle, Great Britain were to be divested of all saleable assets, so that after the victory was won with our blood, civilisation saved, and the time gained for the United States to be fully armed against all eventualities, we should stand stripped to the bone. Such a course would not be in the moral or the economic interests of either of our countries". This plea resonated with President Roosevelt who came to believe it was in the US's best interest to support the war effort to defeat the Nazis without once again saddling allied nations with crippling and politically destabilising post-war debts.

The following year in his lend-lease speech, Robert Menzies was also clearly considering the post-war world. A world war makes us a world nation; not a parochial community, but a world community. Nothing so contributes to peace among men as the maintenance of ordinary, decent commercial relations, and these relations can be restored only by the most liberal statesmanship when the war is over.

Over USD 50 billion (USD 700 billion in today's equivalent) was spent by the US under the Lend-Lease arrangements. While Lend Lease ceased in 1945, the US government under the Truman Doctrine continued to provide Post-war reconstruction support in political, military and economic assistance to democratic nations they deemed to be under threat from authoritarian regimes.

In 1947, Secretary of State George Marshall justified the continuation of this support for what was to become the Marshall Plan. In this speech he described the dysfunction of the European economy and presented a rationale for US aid to promote European recovery and reconstruction:

> The modern system of the division of labour upon which the exchange of products is based is in danger of breaking down. ... Aside from the demoralising effect on the world at large and the possibilities of disturbances arising as a result of the desperation of the people concerned, the consequences to the economy of the United States should be apparent to all.

What Menzies, Churchill and Roosevelt clearly understood is both economic prosperity and security were required for democratic stability. George Marshall captured this in his 1947 speech:

> It is logical that the United States should do whatever it is able to do to assist in the return of normal economic health to the world, without which there can be no political stability and no assured peace. Its purpose should be the revival of a working economy in the world so as to permit

the emergence of political and social conditions in which free institutions can exist.

Unsordid acts can also lead to unforeseen outcomes. One such outcome of the Lend-Lease Act was the emergence of Reverse Lend-Lease, where recipients provided in-kind goods and services back to the US. Reverse Lend-Lease was so successful with the US's Australia and New Zealand allies, by the end of the war, both had contributed more back in-kind that they had received. Australia stored millions of tonnes of US war supplies; they provided US troops with millions of kilos of food, blankets, socks, shoes and military clothing. Australian industry also build US barracks, airfields, hospitals and provided landing craft, vehicles and communications equipment. Friends helping friends.

As Menzies said in 1942, in our democracy we often take too much for granted. Dealing with immediate problems, while planning for the future, is just as important today as it was in the 1940s:

> Looked at in this way, this great lend-lease movement, though for the moment it appears to solve great problems, will produce even greater ones, which it will be one of the principal tasks of post-war statesmanship to overcome.

The legacy of the little known *Lend-Lease Act* extends well beyond the Marshall Plan. One of the enduring lessons for Australian democracy arising from the Lend Lease Act is the necessity to deal with the problems of today, whilst ensuring we keep a close eye on the future. It also reminds us that aid can be an important instrument of national power, particularly when in support of allies.

Australia's future is still a shared one with our Liberal Democrat friends and allies. A future in which our economic and security requirements remain inextricably linked. No matter the irritations and distractions that occur from time to time in all democracies, we must never forget that these are the nations who share our values and with whom we have developed mutual trust and genuine friendships. Friends we can rely on.

These relationships have held fast through two world wars, subsequent conflicts and now together we fight the insurgents who seek to destroy our very way of life.

Robert Menzies exhortation for Australians not just to sits but also to sits and thinks on matters of importance to Australian democracy is just as important today as it was in 1942.

To endure, Democracy must continue to deliver both economic prosperity and security. History will record this Liberal Democratic alliance to be an astonishing and far-sighted shared commitment to the present and to our shared democratic future. It is what Robert Menzies warned Australians never to take for granted.

One Australians must now work hard to ensure it endures.

14

WOMEN IN WAR

Peta Credlin

Three-quarters of a century ago, Robert Menzies was ahead of his times when it came to understanding the role of women in our national political life. Today, we are behind our times and we should consider what we can learn from Menzies because if we don't, we threaten the very electoral viability of the Liberal Party of Australia.

A few months before his landmark Forgotten People address, Robert Menzies delivered a radio broadcast on "Woman at War". It was 20 February 1942. Pearl Harbour had been bombed, the "impregnable fortress" of Singapore had fallen and Darwin had just been devastated, indeed the very day before his broadcast went to air. War had come to Australia. It was no longer a foreign battle that Australia's menfolk had gone away to fight; it now threatened home and hearth.

As Menzies saw it, the mobilisation of women, the "fighting daughters of their country", was the key to the defence of Australia. He believed women had a new role to play if the war was to be won. In earlier conflicts, most women remained in the private realm of their homes while some took on nursing roles but largely, war work remained a male domain, particularly because the vast extent of Australia's participation occurred on foreign soil. With multiple fighting fronts, the sophistication of modern warfare, and not least the lost generation of young men killed in the Great War, the 1942 war effort could no longer operate without the labour of women. 'When I use the expression "man power", I mean man power and not woman power. Plainly, we do not have ample man power for (our) ... needs in light of the new and extending and pressing demands of this war", Menzies said.

Conservatives are pragmatists and it wasn't lofty idealism that drove Menzies to advocate for the right of women to join the war effort. Instead, his advocacy for a shift in societal thinking came from the position of the realist; "On no question", he said, "is a realistic approach so necessary, but so rare, as it is on the question of war employment of women."

Menzies had just returned from Britain where he'd witnessed first-hand the work of women in the war effort. He'd seen how women were working for the good of the state and not just the family; how they'd been released from the bonds of home and children to be a part of something bigger than themselves. He must have sensed as well how doing something for their country in its darkest hour had inspired and invigorated the women of Britain.

In his broadcast, Menzies didn't pretend that their war work would be safe or womanly. He wanted women in the thick of it – as fire-fighters, like those in London's blitz, "not merely standing around and looking picturesque but working hard and fast." He wanted to see women "playing a part worthy of any brave man"; "using riveting machines, wielding hammers, doing in many instances downright hard manual labour."

It was necessity not tokenism; the phrase 'pragmatism based on values' comes to mind.

For his time, Menzies had a remarkably advanced view of the role and the capability of women. Two years after this broadcast, he established the Liberal Party of Australia, with the support of the Australian Women's National League and its large, merged female membership. To this day, in Victoria, the impact of the AWNL alliance remains visible in the formalised gender equality of party organisational positions. Menzies broke ground. He wasn't reacting to a worldwide feminist movement, or a groundswell of activism. Instead, he involved women throughout the party structure because of the impact they could make: on votes, volunteers and the organisational machine that is essential to successful campaign politics.

It's worth remembering that the first woman to sit in an Australian parliament, Edith Cowan, came from the conservative side of politics. The first woman in the House of Representatives, elected 75 years ago this year, was a Liberal too, Dame Enid Lyons; as was the first woman minister.

From its beginning, the Liberal Party has been a vehicle for the empowerment of women – and why wouldn't this be the case when, after all, we are a party where opportunity and individual exceptionalism sit at the very core of our beliefs.

As always, our challenge is to retain the spirit of Menzies in a contemporary political movement.

While the work of Liberal women still keeps the Liberal Party alive at the grassroots level, the weight of female engagement inside the party has not been reflected in female representation in our parliaments. The party of Menzies has forgotten one of the keys to his political success and this amnesia is damaging the party today. If it's not urgently arrested, it will make electoral success much more elusive in the future.

Despite a once proud record, only 22.6 per cent of Liberal members and senators are female while 44 per cent of Opposition MPs are women. Even worse, of the 76 Coalition MPs in the House of Representatives, only 13 are women (12 Liberals and 1 LNP). That's a significant decline from the high-water mark of 17

Liberal women in 1996; and 16 – under John Howard in 2001 and, again, 12 years later under Tony Abbott. With even a modest swing against the Government, the number of Coalition women in the lower house will fall from 13 into single figures and this hasn't been the case since Paul Keating was prime minister.

If you lose your pipeline of women in Opposition, it severely impacts your ministry in government. Without women candidates, you don't get women MPs and without women MPs, you don't get women in Cabinet where the big decisions are made. And when governments lose elections, because women hold so few safe seats, the pipeline is lost too. It's simple electoral arithmetic but I'm always surprised how many observers fail to appreciate that losing experienced women means starting all over again. And once you do return to government, as the Coalition did in the 2013 landslide, it means more women – sure – but newly arrived, so they tend to lose out in the ministry contest to more experienced colleagues who have done the hard-yards in opposition.

According to the Mackerras pendulum, at present, the Coalition has seven women in 'safe to fairly safe' federal seats. On the Opposition side, there are 16 women in the 'safe-to-fairly-safe' cohort. By my reckoning, a three and half per cent swing at the next election would reduce the Coalition's total female ranks in the House of Representatives to seven.

With just over half the electorate female, it's clear that something's got to change.

According to analysis by the Menzies Research Centre of data in the Australian Electoral Survey, at the last election, just 35 per cent of women voted for the Liberal-National Coalition. In 2013, the Coalition's share of the national female vote was a whole ten points higher at 45 and even against the first female prime minister in the 2010 race, the Coalition managed 41. In fact, at every election since the ANU's Professor Ian MacAlister started this post-election voting analysis 30 years ago, the Liberal-National vote share for women has always been above 40.

We need to face the painful but unequivocal truth: the Liberal Party, and the broader Coalition has a problem with women. It is not enough to point to our early and fine history, or to the fact that we have had a female deputy leader for the past decade. It isn't enough.

We need more Coalition women in our branches, in pre-selections, on ballot papers, in our parliaments, and in our ministries and cabinets.

Getting more Liberal women into our state and federal parliaments is a critical step to broadening the Coalition's appeal and stemming the attrition of the overall female vote.

Women make up half the voting population and unless the Coalition can arrest the slide in the female vote, it can't hold government – it is that simple. Some have claimed this is identity politics. It isn't. It's just good politics.

So how does it boost the number of women in the parliament when the conservative parties have been talking about this for decades?

I'm proud of the fact that on the conservative side of politics, women have been promoted because they were the best candidate and not because of a quota. In his remarks following the first speech of Dame Enid Lyons, Prime Minister Curtin said, "now in each chamber of this Commonwealth Parliament a woman sits, sits not because she is a woman, but because she has been elected by the people of Australia." While the other side might have changed its view since Curtin's time, I feel politics is hard enough without the burden of only being there because of a special rule, so I continue to oppose quotas.

But with only 13 Coalition women in the federal lower house, I can't defend the status quo either.

Menzies used the term 'qualified women' and I use it too. Just installing a woman in a seat is no guarantee of success. A dud is a dud regardless of gender and there have been plenty of them on both sides of politics – male and female. Being a woman shouldn't protect you from assessments of competence either. But a qualified candidate is just that and a qualified candidate is your best chance to win.

Julie Bishop often cites the words attributed to former US Secretary of State Madeleine Albright: "there's a special place in hell for women who don't support women". In the six years' I worked as chief of staff to our party's federal leader, I never known a woman to advocate for another woman; never, not once. Yet twice, I had two male ministers push the case for the promotion of a female colleague. As women, sometimes we are our worst enemy.

Today the Coalition is committed to a target of 50/50 female representation by 2025. This target was first championed by Prime Minister Abbott and backed in by Prime Minister Turnbull.

But a target delivers little unless it's got teeth. That means published milestones to ensure accountability, an organisational structure to support women to run and prepare them for the pre-selection process, as well a determination to ensure every pre-selection has a good percentage of women in the field. Unless we're prepared to invest in women, the current target will be nothing more than an excuse for failure as we've all heard too many times – "yes the Liberal Party must do better, but we've at least got a new target."

I want to see the Liberal Party establish a national body to drive the pre-selection of women and work with our divisions to achieve the 50/50 by 2025 target. I believe the body should be affiliated closely to party divisions because it's the state executives that hold the preselection cards, not the national entity but it should have a measure of independence so that it can hold the federal executive and state counterparts to account. Funding will be key to its fearlessness and I have no doubt bodies that find it hard to donate to political parties per se would be more likely to support a body charged with increasing the participation of women in public life.

The body should be representative and it should report progress – publicly – twice a year. The Party is being scrutinised so it might as well own the process. If nothing is done, the Party's vote will continue to suffer damage as women move away. This attrition is unsustainable, it's dumb politics and it's got to reversed.

There's only been four occasions since the Second World War where the Liberal Party has won government from opposition. In 2010 and 2013, the Coalition won 25 seats, the most successful opposition in history because it had the foundations right.

To be serious about electing more women, the foundations have to be right here too. The Party has to find the best talent from the broadest reaches of our communities to reflect the people it seeks to represent.

Potential women candidates need to know how to prepare for a pre-selection, how to advocate policy, how to campaign, how to perform in the media, how to build a supporter base, how to capitalise on local issues, how to fight, and how to win. Whether male or female, the Party needs the best candidates in every race because that's the best chance of winning government. But that requires women in safe seats too to build and protect a ministerial pipeline. Without real targets then I fear quotas might become inevitable in order to avoid ever-reducing electoral irrelevance – and that would not be in the best interests of women or the Liberal Party.

The Party needs a well-funded, national body to champion the election of Liberal women. It cannot set a target for eight years' time and fail to reach it. It cannot afford to drop even lower than a 35 per cent share of the national women's vote – but that will be hard to avoid if female representation falls below double figures in the House of Representatives. This issue won't take care of itself.

As Robert Menzies said in 1942, "there is no reason why a qualified woman should not sit in Parliament, or on the Bench or in a professorial Chair or preach from the pulpit, or if you like, command an army in the field."

These were extraordinary remarks for the time, and dare I say it, for the conservative side of politics which is often perceived as being slow to advance women.

Let's not forget Menzies' lesson, or our history. It shouldn't need to take a world war for Liberal women to learn how to fight.

15
PAYING FOR THE WAR

Christopher Rath

Kids these days have never had it better. My generation, 'the millennials', have never had to go to war, never experienced a recession, and never lived in fear of nuclear holocaust, plague or poverty. Almost 40 per cent of us attend university. Our average life expectancy will reach close to one hundred. Global news and an abundance of information is at our fingertips. We will change careers multiple times, probably more regularly than we change our coffee order or favourite brunch spot. We will travel the world and soon be using driverless vehicles. And as we enter the fourth industrial revolution we will start new businesses in fields not yet imagined and most of us will never have to take on old-style back-breaking jobs. We are a lucky generation and we probably should remember that more often.

Australia has experienced 27 years of unbroken economic growth meaning that my generation has either not lived through or can't remember a recession. During this exact same period we have grown up knowing America as the only superpower with the Soviet Union disintegrating in 1991. Sure there have been global conflicts, but it has been a relatively peaceful world when you think of the two world wars and battle against global communism that previous generations lived through.

We should never forget that our older generations built this great nation of ours. Many fought and died to protect the country they loved and the unique way of life we still enjoy today but so often take for granted. We should remember their achievements and their sacrifice. I am a classical liberal because I believe that my generation should be free to reach our full potential without being punished by excessive government debt, taxes and regulations. But I am also a conservative because I want to conserve the institutions and values that our older generations fought for. John Howard summed this up best when he said "a conservative is someone who does not think he is morally superior to his grandfather."

Every generation wants their children to grow up in a world even better than their own. We strive to improve the world and preserve those things we love so that the next generation may also experience them. Our reasons for this are emotional and virtuous not just rational. We are not just rational sentient beings trying to increase our utility by exchanging good and services. We're also part of a society, one which develops slowly and organically overtime and which is handed down from generation to generation. This is what Edmund Burke meant when he said that society is much more than just a contract between individuals, it is "a partnership not only between those who are living, but between those who are living, those who are dead, and those who are to be born."

We are custodians of this world for only a brief time and while we inherited a natural environment, an economy, institutions, culture, society, and way of life from our parents, we must also preserve and improve on this for the next generation. This partnership between the generations is so special that Burke argued that it must "be looked on with other reverence; because it is not a partnership in things subservient only to the gross animal existence of a temporary and perishable nature. It is a partnership in all science; a partnership in all art; a partnership in every virtue, and in all perfection."

My generation owes a lot to all of those who came before us and no amount of gratitude will ever be enough for the great nation we have inherited. However, there is an imbalance in this inheritance that has the potential to leave my generation poorer and less free than the generation before me unless drastic measures are taken. This intergenerational inequity is being caused by the fact that it has been almost a decade now since Australia last ran a budget surplus. We should always give the Howard/Costello Government immense credit for their fiscal prudence, however successive governments since then have left millennials with Commonwealth Net Debt at $341bn in June 2018.

This is an issue of intergenerational equity because my generation will need to pay back the huge debt incurred today. We will have lower growth, lower incomes, and lower standards of living in the future as a result of the profligacy of today needing to be paid back tomorrow. Government debt is essentially a transfer payment from the young and not yet born to the older generation currently in power. The full effects of this transfer won't be felt for many years and will either be a slow squeeze on our future lifestyles to fund the lifestyles of today or the debt will continue to accumulate to a Greek style crisis point where we are on the brink of being forced to default.

Harvard Professor Niall Ferguson explains that intergenerational debt is an "unparalleled breach of precisely that partnership" that Edmund Burke outlined. Surely it is unfair that my generation will either have to bear the brunt of significantly highly taxes or drastic cuts in government spending just to keep on top of government liabilities? Budget cuts and higher taxes also significantly reduce aggregate demand meaning fewer jobs and a lower growth economy into the future.

The debt problem however is even worse than the figures suggest due to an ageing population. Not only is debt currently being accumulated and passed on to my generation but there will be relatively fewer taxpayers in the future paying for a greater number of elderly Australians requiring pensions, healthcare, aged care, and other social services. The 2015 Intergenerational Report highlights this best by using the dependency ratio. In 1975 there were 7.3 working aged people aged 15 to 64 for every retirement age Australian aged over 65. That figure is currently 4.5 and will steadily decline to just 2.7 by 2055. So not only will millennials and even generations after us be burdened with a huge debt, but will we actually ever be able pay down the debt due to fewer taxpayers paying for more dependents in the economy?

Of course it can be done and indeed has been done before, but considerable sacrifices are required. Niall Ferguson in his book *The Great Degeneration* explains that perhaps the most successful deleveraging in recorded history was after the Napoleonic Wars where debt in Britain stood at over 250 per cent. The Government ran consistent peacetime surpluses over several decades and was also fortunate enough to be presiding over a high growth economy with low interest rates. However, running consistent surpluses was not an easy task as harsh austerity measures led to social unrest in the mid-1820s and late 1840s and was partly responsible for the disastrous famine in Ireland.

In a similar way Sir Robert Menzies' 1942 Forgotten People Speech on Paying for the War called on all Australians to make incredible financial sacrifices for the war effort. He explained that: "In brief, a war effort is a subtraction from normal civil effort. We cannot have it both ways. We cannot have our cake and eat it too. That is why the Government must ask us to go without things we normally buy, if we are to have those military things without which we cannot fight."

The sacrifice shown by Australians during World War II sadly is not being emulated today where every time the Government adopts a new saving measure they are virtually forced to backflip due to community outrage; think of the 2014-15 Federal Budget as the best example.

The alternative to reducing spending is to drastically increase taxes. Again this is unpopular and anathema to classical liberals and conservatives. Millennials won't be able to display any semblance of personal responsibility if they're seeing 65 per cent of their income taken away in taxes to pay for the debt of previous generations. There is no easier way to destroy Menzies' "dynamic middle-class- the strivers, the planners, the ambitious ones" than through higher taxes.

Today it has become all too popular to call for budget repair with policies comprising of only higher taxes on wealthier Australians and big corporations. It needs to be better explained that these policies harm low-income earners the most, as they will see their job move offshore where corporations and entrepreneurs can enjoy lower taxes. We should also remind those arguing for higher taxes that less than 0.1 per cent of corporates account for over 59 per cent of Australia's company tax revenue and less than 9 per cent of individuals pay 47 per cent of Australia's income tax. We should heed the advice of Menzies in 1942 when he warned against increasing taxes on the already overtaxed "big men" to pay for the war. We cannot tax ourselves into prosperity.

So we are left in a quandary as the only way to avoid handing over a huge debt to the next generation is through drastically cutting spending but the political will simply doesn't exist. Older Australians rail against any changes to pensions, social services, healthcare or aged care. But us millennials also find it difficult to compute our own long-term economic interests; we don't really view intergenerational debt as a huge problem and certainly not an immediate one. Unsurprisingly we're much more concerned about university, finding a job, and how we're ever going to afford a home, especially in Sydney where house prices have increased over 70% in the last five years.

We need to start winning the narrative on intergenerational

debt, beginning with millennials who have the most to gain from addressing this issue. However it remains that my generation will also need to convince a significant portion of our parents and grandparents too. The reason for this is demography, recently outlined by Nick Cater:

> In 1975, when Whitlam lost power, 40 per cent of eligible voters were under 35. The over-55s commanded just 25 per cent of the vote. Now the tables have been turned. For the first time, the over-55s were the largest cohort in last year's election, commanding more than 35 per cent of the vote. The millennials' share was a little more than 30 per cent.

No doubt a herculean effort is required to convince older Australians that intergenerational equity is a bigger and more important issue than funding all current and projected social security entitlements. We cannot fall into the trap of short termism and populism. We cannot blame the left for not addressing this issue as their instincts are always of higher taxes, more spending, increased regulations, and spiralling debt. It's in our DNA as conservatives and classical liberals to live within our means and protect the partnership between the generations. Our Party must keep fighting. It's our responsibility and we must show leadership, as nobody else will.

16

POST-WAR PLANNING

Paul Fletcher

After he became Prime Minister in 2015, Malcolm Turnbull appointed a federal Minister for Cities – a first for a federal Coalition Government. Announcing the appointment, the Prime Minister explained his thinking thus:

> Liveable, vibrant cities are absolutely critical to our prosperity. Historically the Federal Government has had a limited engagement with cities and yet that is where most Australians live, it is where the bulk of our economic growth can be found ... We have to ensure for our prosperity, for our future, for our competitiveness, that every level of Government works together, constructively and creatively to ensure that our cities progress.

Just as Menzies articulated new priorities for a Coalition Government in a changing post war world, so his successor Prime Minister has articulated a new priority for a federal Coalition Government: a much greater focus on cities and urban infrastructure. He has done so for several reasons.

The first is that – even though we are a small population on a very large continent – today Australia is one of the world's most urbanised countries.

Around 64 per cent of Australians live in our five biggest cities. Around eighty per cent of us live in our top twenty one cities – ranging from Sydney with a population of over five million to Mackay with a population of just over 80,000.

Our Liberal mission is about working to deliver prosperity for all – not the deliberate focus on certain segments of society which we see from our political opponents. A focus on our cities – where so many Australians live – is very much in line with our mission.

If we need to focus on our cities because they are where the majority of Australians live today, it is even more important to plan for the future growth of our cities. Our big cities are expected to continue to grow strongly; indeed today they are growing at a faster rate than our overall population.

By the twenty fifties both Sydney and Melbourne will be cities of eight million people, and Brisbane and Perth will be substantially larger than today. That means we need to work hard so that our cities remain attractive places to live – and efficient and productive places in which to work and do business.

A second reason for a Commonwealth focus on Australia's cities is their importance to our national prosperity. Around 80 per cent of Australia's GDP is generated in cities of more than 100,000 people. In a recent report the Grattan Institute estimated that 10 per cent of GDP is generated in just the few square kilometres constituted by the central business districts of Sydney and Melbourne.

There is a third reason for Turnbull Government to involve itself with cities policy: the manifest gaps in the existing governance arrangements for our cities. No one council has coverage of our big cities: the Lord Mayors of Sydney and Melbourne for example have responsibility for relatively small areas at the centre of these two cities. At the same time state governments are responsible for large numbers of people beyond the capital cities of each state and so cannot have a single-minded focus on the capital city.

This is compounded by the lack of co-ordination often seen between the different parts of government responsible for urban planning and for transport planning. It is all too rare to have integrated town planning aligned with the construction of a new railway or freeway.

Often there are multiple local councils along the route, each using a different planning process and not necessarily supporting planning approaches which maximise the public benefit of new transport infrastructure. For example, local councils may resist approving apartments and shopping centres around new railway stations, due to local political pressures.

The Sydney South West Rail Link is a good example. It was built at a cost of $1.8 billion – yet the new Leppington Station which opened in 2015 is still surrounded by fields with little nearby housing or commercial development.

There is a strong case, then, for a greater Commonwealth engagement with Australia's cities.

As to how we engage, the Turnbull Government has clear priorities.

The first is to negotiate and agree 'city deals'. These are arrangements between three levels of government – local, state and federal – to agree on shared policy objectives for a particular city, and in turn to bring together commitments from all three levels of government.

Already, we have agreed city deals for Townsville and Launceston. Both involve a coordinated package of measures designed to boost the urban functioning and economic activity of each city, with Townsville seeing a $100 million Commonwealth commitment to build a new football stadium and Launceston to be transformed through the $130 million Commonwealth investment for the relocation of the University of Tasmania campus to central Launceston.

In March 2018, Prime Minister Turnbull joined with Premier Berejiklian and the mayors of eight Western Sydney councils to announce agreement on a city deal for Western Sydney. This is a long term plan for the development of Western Sydney – with a particular focus on how to maximise the business-attracting, jobs-generating power of the Commonwealth's $5.3 billion investment in Western Sydney Airport.

The deal includes a big focus on land use planning, with the Commonwealth and NSW Governments to work together to plan the Badgerys Creek 'aerotropolis' near the airport – an urban area that will be a hub for sectors such as advanced manufacturing, aerospace, defence, education and skills.

It incorporates major public transport commitments, such as rapid bus services to the airport and the aerotropolis from Liverpool, Campbelltown and Penrith; and a commitment to build the first stage of the North-South rail link from St Mary's to the aerotropolis via the airport. For the first time, we are working with all levels of government to put a plan and the infrastructure in place – ahead of the coming growth in population and housing.

And the deal provides for significant work to be led by the councils, including a planning compact designed to deliver faster building approvals using a consistent framework across the different local council areas.

Over the next twenty years an extra million people are expected to live in Western Sydney. The Western Sydney City Deal sets out an integrated plan, with co-ordinated actions across all three levels of government, to develop an economically thriving and highly liveable city around the economic core of Western Sydney Airport and the new aerotropolis industry precinct.

It brings together substantial infrastructure spending with other policy levers such as land use planning and education policy to stimulate business activity, generate jobs and bring new housing to market.

We have also committed to city deals in a range of other cities including Darwin, Hobart and Geelong, and have work underway to develop the content of these deals. Similar themes arise in these deals too – such as more streamlined and better coordinated approaches to planning, for example through the proposed Greater Hobart Act, which will coordinate planning across the four councils which cover the Hobart metropolitan area.

The use of City Deals as a policy tool is a very practical, Liberal way of overcoming some of the problems of our federation. We know all too well the problems of multiple levels of government, confusion about responsibilities and the temptation for politicians to engage in cost and blame shifting.

Rather than searching for a grand solution as some academics propose, we are rolling up our sleeves and working on the practical issues, city by city. City Deals let us identify the problems we need to solve; work out a plan involving all three levels of government; and then enter into a deal where each level of government gives a formal commitment about the actions it will take towards solving those problems.

City Deals recognise the autonomy of each level of government; they are a framework to deliver nation building infrastructure; and they draw together many of our economic and social goals because we are a nation of communities and not just economies.

The Turnbull Government's focus on nation building is very much in the Menzies tradition. The infrastructure investments we are making – be it Western Sydney Airport, or the Bruce Highway in Queensland, or the transformed university and central city area in Launceston – will deliver benefits for twenty, fifty or a hundred years into the future.

As Sir Robert said of national development under his government: "There can never be anything static about a policy of national development; that would be a contradiction in terms … It is not enough for us as a Government or as a nation, to say: "We have lived!" We must feel the excitement of living and working and planning and building."

Our task is to continue the efforts of work, planning and building so that we make it easier for Australians to thrive and prosper in our cities.

We are doing this by taking a much more proactive approach to the way the Commonwealth funds and supports urban transport infrastructure. In 2018-19 the Turnbull Government will invest some ten billion dollars in infrastructure around the country, with much of that to be spent in our largest cities.

In making these investments the Turnbull Government has a strong focus on infrastructure which will help our cities function more effectively. Projects like the $16.8 billlion WestConnex in Sydney (which includes $3.5 billion in funding and financing from the Turnbull Government), transformation of the North South Corridor in Adelaide (with $1.6 billion of Commonwealth funding towards three major projects including the 15.5 kilometre Northern Connector), upgrades to the M1 and Gateway North motorways in South East Queensland, the Tullamarine Freeway and M80 Ring Road in Melbourne and Northlink in Perth are vital to helping people move around our cities as quickly and efficiently as possible. WestConnex for example will reduce the time taken to travel from Parramatta to Sydney Airport by 40 minutes.

Our infrastructure investment also includes a strong emphasis on public transport. We have committed $1.7 billion to Sydney Metro City and Southwest, a metro style rail line which will run from Chatswood in the north to Bankstown in the south west over a combination of new and upgraded track. In Perth, there is major investment occurring in new rail lines, and the Commonwealth has contributed $490 million to the new Perth to Forrestfield Airport rail link and committed $700 million for the planned Thornlie to Cockburn line and the Yanchep Line extension.

New investment in rail in and around our big cities will continue for years to come. In last year's budget we announced our plan to spend ten billion dollars over the next ten years on transformational rail projects in our big cities and their surrounding regional areas.

New rail lines have a very big impact on the development of cities. If we want to shape the future of our cities, building more rail lines is a very effective tool.

Similarly we are using transformative rail investment to underpin the economic growth of our regions – whether it is our $8.4 billion equity investment in Inland Rail or the $1.45 billion we have committed for regional rail projects in Victoria, including upgrades to lines running from Melbourne into regional areas.

As our cities grow larger, we are seeing big changes in the distribution of jobs and housing. Increasingly knowledge economy jobs are concentrating in central business districts and in employment hubs such as Macquarie Park in Sydney and around the campuses of Melbourne University and Monash University in Melbourne.

To serve such employment hubs, we need transport systems capable of moving large numbers of people quickly, something rail is well suited for. A metro style rail line can move up to 50,000 people an hour – by contrast a single freeway lane will move around 2,000 people in the same time period.

As we build out new rail and road backbones for our cities, it is vital that we integrate our approaches to land use and transport planning. This is where the use of city deals offers an opportunity to bring together a more integrated approach, across all three levels of government.

Of course it is also important that such development comes with high standards of amenity. If more Australians are to live in apartments and townhouses, as our cities grow larger, it is important that they have ready access to community facilities such as libraries and childcare centres; to shops, restaurants and cafes; and of course to parks and recreation spaces for both children and adults.

We understand that as our cities grow, the best way to keep pressure off ever-increasing property prices is to increase the supply of housing. Our approach is to to encourage an integrated planning approach for our major cities which sees an increased supply of apartments and townhouses, particularly along transport corridors and around rail stations; and which sees such areas well supported with community facilities and parks and recreation spaces.

We are working with state and local governments on such approaches – including by attaching conditions to our infrastructure funding, and by specifying such approaches as part of city deals. State and local governments, for their part, are delivering some impressive outcomes.

Our third priority is to integrate our approach to cities with policy levers in a range of other areas.

Menzies argued that the foundation of the nation is in our homes. The ethos of "homes material, homes human and homes spiritual" is at the heart of our party. The foundation of this ethos is ensuring as many Australians as possible have the opportunity to own their own home. This is particularly important in our biggest cities where there is continued upward pressure on house prices.

The Turnbull Government is pursuing a range of measures to address this, including allowing people who are saving for a deposit to use their superannuation fund to do so (meaning that savings can build up more quickly thanks to the lower tax on superannuation) and giving superannuation incentives for older Australians to downsize from large family homes, freeing up capacity for the next generation.

But we are also coordinating these policies with measures to increase the supply of land for housing – recognising that housing affordability pressures in large measure emerge from the supply of new housing not keeping up with demand in our biggest cities. For example, in the 2017 Budget the Turnbull Government announced that 127 hectares of Department of Defence land in Maribrynong in inner western Melbourne would be sold, opening up Melbourne's largest remaining urban infill redevelopment site. It is clear that we need a renewed focus on our cities. They must remain pleasant and liveable; they need to function efficiently and allow people to move around as quickly as possible; and they play a vital role in our nation's economic performance.

Historically cities and urban infrastructure policy has not been seen as a priority by federal Coalition governments. But just as Menzies moved to have the federal government engage with a new range of concerns in post war Australia, so Prime Minister Turnbull has sought to focus his government on this policy area of high and growing importance in our highly urbanised modern nation.

17
THE RATIONALISATION OF INDUSTRY

Jane Hume

No responsible government should ever be completely beholden to its most ideological elements. In a democracy where all voices are heard and weighed, principled pragmatism over policy purity is a reality government inevitably faces.

Throughout the last seventy-five years, in both development and delivery of policy, Liberal leaders have reiterated this most Burkean of principles – "Circumstances give in reality to every political principle its distinguishing colour and discriminating effect".

No more so do we see this paradox than in the relationship between economics and politics which has forever been inexorable but uncomfortable. The Smithian purists among us contend that a market free from government interference is the most efficient and will generate the best outcomes. But even Adam Smith recognised that markets – made up of individuals imbued with human frailties – do not operate in a vacuum and that there is a role for government in economies and societies.

Politics and economics do, however, speak as one on the imperative for low unemployment. This is why, beyond national security and the safety of its citizenry, the creation of more jobs is the core objective of any responsible government.

The primacy of employment growth is always a feature of Coalition governments – the Howard years saw an additional 2.3 million jobs created.

At the time of print, the Coalition government has overseen the generation of one million new jobs in less than two terms of government. Over 1,100 jobs per day have been generated in the last twelve months alone, two-thirds have been full-time. The majority of new jobs went to women. Around a hundred thousand were in regional Australia. Importantly, the participation rate – the most instructive indicator of the economic benefits of low unemployment – is at its highest rate in seven years.

The enormity of this achievement cannot be understated.

These jobs have been generated as our commodity sensitive economy emerges from a one-in-a-hundred-years mining investment boom. It is an act of economic defiance and national resilience, but it is not an accident. Luck is not a policy platform.

While the Coalition should be proud of its record, we remain acutely aware that governments don't create jobs. The private sector – businesses – create jobs.

It is government's role to get the settings right and to respond to the circumstances of the day. To encourage businesses to invest, grow and employ people in more and higher paying jobs, government priorities must be to lower taxes and other costs of doing business, remove red tape, ensure flexibility in workplace practices, and, ultimately, generate opportunities.

Generation of opportunities comes in many guises. It could be through the negotiation of free trade agreements such as those with China, South Korea, Japan and the soon to be completed Trans Pacific Partnership (TPP). These bilateral and multilateral treaties remove barriers to international trade and investments, opening up new markets to Australian businesses and presenting unprecedented opportunities for business expansion. Liberalised trade gives our producers, manufacturers and services providers better access to and demand from billions of consumers across the globe, not just the 25 million who call Australia home. The results of the Coalition's free trade agreements on business growth and job creation have been significant.

It's important to remember that, while contemporary Liberals feel that free trade is a part of our DNA, it has not always been thus. Early Liberals of the Deakinite tradition were innately protectionist, as was Menzies himself. The circumstances of the Menzies era gave the Liberal principles and polices their Burkean "distinguishing colour and discriminating effect" just as contemporary circumstances do today. Free trade agreements are a policy application of a Liberal principle that reflects the changing global circumstances.

The role of government in generating opportunities for businesses to grow, invest and employ has the potential to be more controversial. Smithian free market purists warn governments away from 'picking winners'. The idea of subsidising industries with 'corporate welfare', particularly inefficient industries, draws the ire of Liberals.

In an increasingly globalised world that is changing rapidly with the advent of new technologies, and a country that is transitioning from a commodity reliant economy to a more stable broad based economy, Australia is faced with a set of extraordinary circumstances.

How does a responsible government best place the economy to take advantage of opportunities and mitigate risks? What sort of policy agenda should a responsible government develop and deliver to to establish core industry competencies in the new economy? How can government act to position businesses to take advantage of change rather than suffer at its hands? Importantly, how do we ensure that, wherever possible, no one is left behind?

Extraordinary times demand more than ordinary policy.

A key component of the Coalition's economic plan is a practical focus on science and technology. Unlike traditional industry policy initiatives, science and technology permeates through other portfolios vital to economic progress such as education, health, energy, environment and small business. Innovation, digital adoption and technological change can be applied to Australia's traditional economic strengths – mining, agriculture, medical and financial services – to generate sustainable economic growth, and to create and secure more jobs.

When politicians speak about innovation, we often inadvertently frighten people. When they hear about game changing innovations like artificial intelligence, robotics, blockchain, the internet of things – many Australians feel threatened by what they don't understand rather than see opportunity. But part of the message must be that the benefits of innovation, of science and of technology extend far beyond those who wear white coats to work, those who have more degrees than a thermometer, those who can code, or millennial "appreneurs".

There is a ripple effect in the economy that flows from our success in science and technology.

Almost 80 percent of Australians are now employed in service sector jobs. A decade ago, growth in high-skilled creative jobs officially took the lead in employment share and has grown to occupy a 36 percent share of the labour market. These jobs are paid around 40 percent more on average than other jobs and are growing at a faster pace. These are the jobs that rely directly and indirectly on innovation, science and technology.

However, these jobs often occur in companies and industries that are mobile and that respond to policy settings that suit their growth strategy. There are plenty of countries who compete to innovate, digitise and commercialise science and research that would happily vie for the industries, companies, jobs and wages that can create a sustainable economy for future generations.

In times of seismic change – such as global war in the Menzies era or the technological revolution in the global economy today – there is an imperative for government to participate in markets to provide opportunity for the progress of industry, productivity and jobs of the future.

One such initiative is establishment of Industry Growth Centres, which drive innovation, productivity and competitiveness by focusing on areas of competitive strength and strategic priority. These centres are collaborative and industry-led, but supported by government networks and resources, and the objective is to grow excellence, not dependence, in industries of the future such as cyber security, advanced manufacturing, food and agribusiness, medical technologies, mining equipment and technology, and energy resources.

These are the industries in which the demand for jobs is growing. They are the industries that provide the ripple effects to the wider economy, and that will effect the transition from a commodity dependent economy to a more stable, broader-based economy with greater resilience, more opportunities for growth, and more and better paying jobs.

Menzies recognised that a responsible government must be courageous enough to respond to significant events even if those responses are not always popular, but equally a responsible government should never use a crisis to further an ideological agenda.

Australia is indeed experiencing a seismic shift, and in the Menzian spirit, such times demand courageous government. Importantly, there is no ideological opportunism in the Liberal response; the creation of jobs in a growing economy should be the prime objective of governments of all hues.

Low unemployment is an efficient use of resources and leads to higher standard of living. It increases tax revenue allowing for better delivery of social services like health and education. These are the economic arguments. But there is so much more that high levels of employment provides. Government strives for job creation because it makes not just for a better economy, but for a better society.

People who are employed are less likely to commit a crime. Employed people have better health outcomes. Women who are financially independent are less likely to experience domestic violence. Rates of illicit drug use are higher among the unemployed. Children's cognitive and social outcomes are lower in families with persistent joblessness. The correlations are irrefutable.

An economy that provides opportunity for employment of its citizens creates a society in which those citizens can flourish.

That is what Menzies Liberalism is all about – an opportunity for every citizen to become their best selves.

18

TAXING THE SHAREHOLDER

Kelly O'Dwyer

Of all public policies taxation stands out as the hardest and most contentious.

Everybody believes they pay too much tax including those who pay no tax, and among the loudest voices in the choir beseeching government to impose new and higher taxes, are groups that are tax exempt – unions, charities, churches, and other non-government organisations.

And yet, as Robert Menzies showed us back in World War II, tax conversations like all other policy conversations also boil down to values, because values are at the heart of all policy choices, and the tax policy we ultimately choose reveals our collective values and aspirations.

For example, we in the Liberal Party believe in the values of freedom, choice and independence – we are free to choose where and how we live; we are free to choose how hard we work and where we spend or invest the fruits of our labour; we believe we are all better off if more of us are independent of government rather than dependent on government.

Menzies would have therefore been alarmed at a pernicious notion about taxation that has arisen in recent decades.

This is that any starting point in the tax debate should encompass the total potential tax take a government could impose on its citizens and then work back from there to see what is an achievable or a reasonable level of taxation.

In its annual tax expenditure statement the Commonwealth Treasury publishes information about concessional or punitive provisions. This can be misunderstood and misused by various vested interest groups to argue that the Federal Government is never taxing enough.

Thus, in their ideal world an Australian Government should tax all capital gains from the proceeds of the sale of the family home, it should tax superannuation more heavily, and the GST could be collected on everything including education, childcare, aged care, health care, and fresh food and vegetables.

Taking this argument to its natural conclusion (as these groups frequently do) is the idea that all private income, all profit, all property and all capital gains belongs to the government, which then in turn "permits" an individual or business or trust to keep a portion of that.

Menzies would have found this idea abhorrent and we, the current custodians of the Liberal Party, would agree with him. We won't inflict a taxation system that would remove the incentive for Australians to strive for greater economic security for themselves and their families.

We believe in the inviolability of private property; that the progress of society depends on the freedom of the individual, and that government should always aim to encourage enterprise and hard work by keeping taxes as low as is possible.

During his wartime wilderness years Menzies confronted a proposal by his political opponents who were in government to severely restrict profits of business to 4 per cent, above which all profits would go to the government.

But Menzies did not argue as a champion of big business:

> I am not a bit concerned to defend the position of the rich. As I've said to you on previous occasions, they can as a rule look after themselves, and their hardships are in any

case relative and not absolute. But I am concerned, and increasingly concerned, with the ordinary middle range of people in this country, those who are not rich and yet, urged on by a spirit of independence, endeavour in spite of every parliamentary discouragement, to provide for their own future.

His response was based on the values he espoused.

Menzies was against over-taxing big business on the grounds of financial justice, the danger of it creating an unbalanced taxation system, and because it was ultimately an attack on what he called "the thrifty and the independent".

Menzies' people (as are the people the Liberal Party champions today) comprised the great bulk of Australians who quietly went about their lives and their businesses, who work hard, pay their taxes and cheerfully contribute to the nation they cherish both monetarily and voluntarily through the communities they live in.

Menzies knew that overtaxing business would ultimately hurt the employees of businesses, the shareholders that were investors in business, the customers of each enterprise, and ultimately the economy of the nation.

Nobody taxes their way to prosperity.

Prosperity is achieved by individual effort and reward for that effort.

The same debate, albeit in different economic and social circumstances, is happening today.

The Turnbull Government has asked the Parliament to act in the national interest and enact our enterprise tax plan to cut the corporate tax rate to 25 per cent.

This is not to give a leg up to big business, but because supporting enterprise leads to a stronger economy, and more jobs and more better-paying jobs.

Opposition to cutting business tax burdens tends to view companies as having an existence separate from those who own them. To be sure, even some policy analysts like the corporate income tax because they think businesses should pay taxes, not people. But the fact that businesses remit payments to the Australian Tax Office doesn't really tell you whose bottom line is affected by it.

It could be the company's shareholders (and superannuants) in lower dividends.

It could be the workers in lower wages.

The tax could be passed through to consumers in the form of higher prices. Or it could be some combination of shareholders, workers and consumers. And yet policy discourse, or what passes for it, pretends that Australians are not hurt by high business taxes.

All taxpayers should be paying the tax they owe to the Australian people – and this is especially true of overseas companies that earn money here.

Any perception that the tax system is unbalanced and unfair erodes tax morale and robs the community of revenue to provide services and a safety net to the vulnerable. Hence the Turnbull Government's strong tax integrity measures, such as the Multinational Anti-Avoidance Law which is already adding more than $7 billion in sales revenue to our tax base annually, and has caused 38 multi-national companies to change their tax affairs.

Those with eyes to see are watching the rest of the world reducing business taxes, including the United States, the United Kingdom, France and Belgium, while business taxes in our region are low and continue to be.

Menzies was an accomplished barrister, not an economist. He well understood that a government should not spend more than it earns, except in times of crisis. Borrowing to finance expenses can lead to the ruin of a household, a business or a nation, without a plan to pay back debt. And lifting taxes as a way of financing a profligate budget can sap a nation's economic lifeblood by removing individual incentive.

The responsibilities of government are vastly more complex than it was at the time Menzies delivered his Forgotten People talks. Successive governments demand taxpayers hand over more of their income in taxes for ever multiplying government programs, bureaucratic oversight of social activities, and myriad of new social welfare benefits for its people.

This can be a challenge. Yet we must never forget that the tax dollar comes from the people and the Government has the responsibility to spend that money wisely and in the national interest.

If there is one lesson to be learned over the recent period of politics, once a program or entitlement is established and legislated it is difficult to unwind, despite the fact that such spending is contributing to deficits and debt. To let the Budget deficit blow out is to burden future generations with higher taxes and diminished opportunities.

The vision of the modern day Liberal Party is to develop a taxation system which seeks to remain internationally competitive, innovative, and also fair.

But it must be grounded in its enduring values of always endeavouring to work for long-term prosperity; that backs individual effort, hard work and independence.

19
HAS CAPITALISM FAILED?

Adam Boyton

With Australia now entering an unprecedented twenty-eighth year of economic growth, the question: "has capitalism failed" would seem much easier to answer today than in 1942.

Especially when we consider what a modern capitalist economy has ultimately been able to provide Australians. After all it is the wealth produced by a modern capitalist economy that funds a social safety net and universal healthcare.

Stepping back seventy five years, however, the question 'has capitalism failed' would have seemed much more reasonable. Indeed, the preceding fifty years had resulted in little improvement in the living standards of Australians. The 1890s had seen a severe depression – indeed on some measures it was a more severe contraction than the depression of the 1930s. The return to normalcy in the aftermath of the 1890s Depression was punctuated by the destruction of the First World War; while the roaring twenties had given way to the Great Depression of the 1930s. The recovery out of that depression was again all too swiftly cut short by the dark clouds of war.

Against that backdrop there is little wonder Menzies chose to ask, and answer, the question.

But seventy five years on from the 1942 broadcasts it is harder to make a case for a similar questioning of capitalism. Australian living standards have risen dramatically over the past seventy five years. One measure – GDP per capita – shows a two hundred and fifty per cent rise since 1942. And business cycles, while they still exist, are much tamer than those that preceded 1942.

Australia is today also arguably much more capitalist than in Menzies' time. Indeed, in the years since the 1942 broadcasts Australians had a determinative say in the 1949 election on bank nationalisation; a decision point that likely denoted the high water mark of socialism in Australia. And while the public sector as a share of GDP back then was much smaller than today (outside the war years, of course), the degree of government intervention, regulation and involvement in the economy would seem excessive by today's standards.

Various changes of government in the post-war years did little to alter the broad structure of the Australian economy. That was until Australia and Australians then spent much of the 1980s, 1990s and early 2000s dismantling the Australian Settlement (as coined by Paul Kelly in his 1992 work The End of Certainty). The economic elements of the Settlement were, in essence, a 'living' wage delivered within a highly structured arbitration and conciliation framework, with business 'protected' from consequent cost of divorcing wages from competitiveness by tariffs barriers.

The legacy of such a structure had become clear by the late 1970s and early 1980s. Australia's living standards had declined relative to other developed economies and large parts of Australian industry were uncompetitive. It was ultimately consumers – Australians – that bore those costs.

With the reform agendas of the 1980s, 1990s and early 2000s sufficiently well-known they do not need repeating in detail here. In essence government businesses were sold, competition introduced into sectors of the economy where there had been none, the currency floated and the labour market progressively deregulated. Since the recession of the early 1990s Australia is subsequently closing in on twenty eight years of uninterrupted economic growth. An extraordinary outcome; unrivalled across the globe.

The legacy of the reforms of the 1980s, 1990s and early 2000s has also seen a recovery in Australia's relative global standing. Indeed – at the height of the mining boom Australian GDP per capita was the fifth highest in the world.

Such a period of growth and a recovery in Australia's global standing would seem to be a vindication of the shift toward a less regulated and more 'capitalist' Australia. Albeit – and as always – appropriately tempered capitalism.

As Menzies himself put it, the choice is not: "between an unrestricted capitalism and a universal socialism. We shall do much better if we keep the good elements of the capitalist system, while at the same time imposing upon capital the most stringent obligations to discharge its social and industrial duty".

Also reflecting the success of capitalism is the fact that the two major political parties in Australia both support a capitalist economy. That support does, of course, prevent disagreement around the extent of intervention in the economy; and disagreement around the nature and degree of redistribution.

So it would seem today that the question of whether or not capitalism has failed in Australia has perhaps already been answered for us. After all, if it was a failure surely there would be an actively debated alternative?

Even if there isn't a clear alternative perhaps it is nonetheless desirable for the exponents of capitalism to question it. The detractors will always point to the negatives: the instances of market failures and questions of inequality. Questioning the basis of our modern economy and society must not be left solely to those who come at the question with nothing more than an ideological opposition.

But what do we mean by capitalism? Menzies viewed it as a "system of social arrangement which recognises and protects private property and encourages and protects private production and business enterprise for profit". Modern dictionary definitions put it as "An economic and political system in which a country's trade and industry are controlled by private owners for profit, rather than by the state" or "a system under which the means of production, distribution, and exchange are in large measure privately owned and directed".

In essence, the common thread to them all is a system of private ownership of the means of production. Yet capitalism is hardly a static concept. It does and has evolved over time. And it is not absolute – we are not here attempting to argue in favour of a system where all of a society's resources are privately controlled.

So where might we argue that capitalism – our economic system – has failed?

Perhaps the global recession of 2009? Signs of rising inequality or inequity at home? Or does globalisation reflect a failure of capitalism? On the latter point, Adam Smith's The Wealth of Nations was in the first instance an attack on mercantilist thinking on international trade before it outlined a framework for a modern market economy.

So does globalisation reflect a failure of capitalism? It might be hard to argue against that proposition in our former manufacturing heartlands. But if we adopt a view of the world that is a little less developed-economy centric, the benefits of globalisation are stark. Through the supply of goods (and also services) to consumers in the West, globalisation has also been behind a reduction in poverty – particularly extreme poverty – across much of the developing world. We should not seek to argue against globalisation and the global reach of capitalism solely through a focus on the impacts across various sectors of the developed economies. To do so ignores that globalisation has delivered to some of the poorest around the globe an extra-ordinary surge in income.

And while the average worker in the United States has not seen an increase in their after inflation wage since the 1970s perhaps that should be considered less an indictment on capitalism and globalisation, but instead more a reflection of the wage bargaining processes and framework at play in that economy. The same, after all, has not been true in Australia over the past forty years where average wages after inflation have risen over fifty per cent since the 1970s; and thirty per cent in the past forty years.

So did the global financial crisis represent a failure of capitalism? While it has certainty presented a challenge to capitalism in other parts of the globe, it is less clear that there was any fundamental failure of capitalism in Australia.

Australia managed, after all, to avoid recession despite what occurred across most of the rest of the world. The combination of aggressive interest rates cuts and an early fiscal stimulus managed to prevent the worst. Critically, when it came to the latter the ability to ward off recession with a massive fiscal stimulus was a function of the stellar budgetary position John Howard and Peter Costello had bequeathed Australia – a budget surplus and zero net debt. And resorting to Keynesian economics to fend off a recession does not reflect a failure of capitalism; rather it reflects a shift in the economics profession since the Great Depression of the 1930s. It also reflects an answer to Menzies' call from 1942 that "we must become better economists in our attack upon the problem of boom and depression".

So perhaps rising inequality reflects a failure of capitalism? We must be honest here. A degree of inequality is part and parcel of capitalism. As Menzies put it, "but however elaborate the machine, it must have a motive power, a driving force. And in a material sense that force, I repeat, must be the urge in the human being to strive for progress and for reward".

The dynamism of capitalism is not found in an equality of outcome. That does not mean we abandon the quest for an equality of opportunity of course. Indeed a well performing capitalist economy actually provides the material basis to deliver that equality of opportunity.

In any event, it appears that concerns around recent increases in income inequality may be overstated. Recent work by the Australian Bureau of Statistics finds that while income inequality did increase from 2003-04 to 2007-08, it has since then "varied within a relatively narrow range".

But what of the successes of capitalism? Perhaps they are so ubiquitous in our modern world that we hardly think of them.

Living standards that generally rise over time and have more than doubled in the seventy five years since 1942.

Innovation, which almost always ends up in the hands of a consumer due to private enterprise. Yes, the internet may have started its life as a US Defence Department program, but it was private enterprise that placed it at the centre of our modern lives. It was private enterprise that placed it in a device in the palm of our hands; and it was private enterprise that turned the knowledge of the world into something called 'search'.

Yet the ultimate success of capitalism must be what the engine of a capitalist economy has enabled us to deliver for the disadvantaged and the less fortunate. A comprehensive social safety net: A National Disability Insurance Scheme, unemployment and sickness benefits, universal access to tertiary education, paid parental leave, and universal healthcare. To name just some.

It is our dynamic capitalist economy that has allowed Australia to provide so much for Australians. Indeed, just as Menzies hoped, a modern and civilised capitalism has contributed much to the modern world.

20

THE DRINK PROBLEM

Alan Tudge

All problems must be seen in their context. 'The Drink Problem' described by Menzies in 1942 appears small relative to the challenges of alcohol and drugs today. Then, temperance was the norm. There were no take-away bottle shops, bars shut at 6pm, and when they did, the men drinking in them tended to go home to their wives and children.

However, as Menzies describes, the Second World War saw an increase in alcohol consumption, which was particularly apparent when the men of the fighting services came home for a few days leave. When this occurred, social standards started to loosen and the community became "a little more noisy, so to speak, in its habits".

This was Menzies core concern; social decay from excess alcohol consumption. This was 'the drink problem'.

Of course, today we are considerably more liberal in relation to alcohol consumption. We accept late-night and early-morning drinking in city and town centres. We drink twice as much as in 1942 and almost three times as much as in 1937.

It would be easy to dismiss, therefore, Menzies' address as irrelevant to today or the future. The times are simply too different, it could be said.

Such a conclusion would be wrong.

To start, we still have a 'drink problem' even if it is different to the public concerns of the early 1940s. We now see too many examples of alcohol fuelled violence on our streets. Many of our remote communities are drowning in grog and causing a breakdown in society. Too many kids are neglected by alcoholic parents.

Just as destructive and serious is the modern scourge of drugs. There are many different drugs that have ruined the lives of young and old. Currently that drug is ice. It has broken families and destroyed lives.

Whether alcohol or drugs, the 'problem' has the same origins: consumption of substances that taken in excess cause problems to not just the individual, but society at large.

Knowing the problem, what might be the solution?

Menzies articulates a framework for how to curb substance abuse. In 'The Drink Problem', he outlines a three-pronged approach: the taking of individual responsibility, the constraining of supply, and the redirection of purchasing power (ie curbing demand). Each of these elements relies on classic conservative and liberal principles and remains relevant to our current substance abuse problems.

Let's examine each in turn.

First, Menzies points out that responsibility ultimately rests with the individual: "the ultimate cure to the abuse of drink is to be found in the character of the individual and his capacity for moderation and self-restraint, self discipline".

While we now know that alcoholism, and addiction generally, can result in a permanent neurological change, the concept of responsibility remains the most important idea to thinking about modern substance abuse and social decay. It is not the only idea, but is a central principle.

It is fundamentally the responsibility of individuals and families to seek assistance if their substance-taking gets out of control. The state can have a role in providing this assistance and encouraging the taking of responsibility (as our drug testing trials do). But we should not fall for the progressive view that substance abuse is a symptom of deeper problems in society and is therefore outside individual and community control.

Where Menzies could have gone further on this key point of personal responsibility is reinforcing the fact that community norms either help or hinder a person taking responsibility.

When heavy drinking or drug taking becomes the social norm in a community, it is harder for even the most disciplined of characters to resist. For example, we see this in remote indigenous communities where, over time, even some of the grandmothers who had been holding the communities together have begun drinking. According to the national drug and alcohol household survey, 50 percent of people take drugs for the first time because of peer-influence. Only 8 percent do so because they are feeling low.

In order to assist with the taking of individual responsibility, we need to maintain healthy social norms and to actively rail against the normalisation of dangerous drinking or drug taking. This is harder than in Menzies day because so much of the social fabric of the mid-century has broken down, particularly the strength of churches and the family. Nevertheless, guiding the establishment of social norms so that people make better decisions must always be an objective of policy makers and community leaders.

Menzies stated that the taking of individual responsibility is the ultimate solution, but he also acknowledged that this was hard to shift immediately. He clearly believed that there was an urgency to the drinking problem – "an insistent demand for reform" – and so he searched for and articulated more immediate solutions. This is why he introduced the second and third parts of his framework: limit supply and curb demand.

Menzies was clearly pragmatic:

> If you bring into connection very large supplies of liquor and very large sums of spare spending money, it is quite inevitable that you will have an increase in drinking and an increase in drunkenness.

The large supply of liquor that Menzies was referring to was a relative one – during the war other products were rationed but liquor was not, although the Government had decided to cut beer production by a third earlier in the year. Menzies supported further supply restrictions.

Supply-side restrictions have always been a key means of limiting social harm from addictive substances. In relation to alcohol, opening hours of the pubs and bars has traditionally been the key restriction, while in gambling and drugs, restricting the products availability generally has been the objective. How far society goes in restricting supply has always been debated and the two strands of Liberal Party thought – liberalism and conservatism – sometimes conflict on this topic.

Undoubtedly the restriction of supply makes an impact. Witness the end of the 1990s heroin epidemic when the supply was cut. Prices consequently spiked and demand dropped. We are endeavouring to do the same with the ice epidemic, but it is far more difficult because the drug is synthetic and easily manufactured. When one supplier shuts down, another opens.

Menzies doesn't provide guidance on how to think about supply-side restrictions and how to get the right balance between individual liberty and protection of harm. Rather his views were pragmatic for the time: there was a problem causing "deplorable social results" and so further restrictions were required. We still restrict the supply of alcohol in every state and territory through limited opening hours of bars and pubs and bottle shops.

The most radical of his ideas was the third element of his framework: limit demand.

Menzies had observed that because of the Second World War, an additional £150 million had suddenly become available to people because of war wages. With more cash and fewer things to spend money on, an increase in drinking was seen by him as inevitable: "having more cash ... they will buy two drinks instead of one, or three drinks instead of two".

Menzies therefore suggested a need to "divert spending power". There "must be a compulsion to frugality", he said.

He did not detail how he was proposing to enact this idea. On one interpretation, he was still referring to enhanced supply restrictions. But it appears from a plain reading of 'The Drink Problem' that he was suggesting that somehow wages should be quarantined so that too much could not be spent on alcohol.

To me, the concept of quarantining earned wages is contrary to a free society. If someone has earned cash from working, then that money should be theirs to spend as they see fit.

Where we can rightly quarantine money is when it is welfare cash.

The use of welfare cash to purchase large volumes of alcohol or drugs was not a concern in Menzies' day – there was full employment and a very small welfare sector. Today, there are communities almost entirely dependent on welfare. In some of these communities, according to one study, half of all the welfare dollars provided were spent on alcohol – with catastrophic social outcomes. Similarly with drug use: a quarter of people on unemployment benefits took drugs last year.

We are now using Menzies' concept of "diverting spending power" to ensure that welfare money is not supporting community harm. With the advancements of technology, we can now provide welfare payments onto a cashless debit card that restricts purchases of alcohol, gambling and drugs. The impact in the original locations where we trialled this has been impressive and now we are rolling it out further. As technology advances, greater targeting of welfare payments will be further enabled.

The drink problems of Menzies' time seem quaint today. But perhaps that makes his prescriptions even more relevant than ever.

21
IS INFLATION A BOGEY?

Louise Ahern

One of the dreary tropes of modern political life is distinguishing the current set of circumstances from every other set of circumstances ever faced by our country.

"This time is different!" goes the chorus; "the past can't help us" goes the verse.

And so it goes with Menzies broadcast "Is inflation a Bogey", which went to air in 1942.

The country was at war and the enemy was close at hand.

Government policy was centered around diverting all available resources to the war effort.

Tariffs enjoyed bipartisan support, subsidies oozed through agriculture and the key drivers of the external economy – the exchange rate and interest rates – were all under government control.

In Australia today, the currency floats, interest rates are determined by the Reserve Bank, agriculture is largely unsubsidised and economists worry about low levels of inflation.

So far, so different.

But imagining ourselves in the turbulence of 1942 and the real risk of catastrophic currency devaluation, with the ruinous unravelling of the German and French currencies still fresh in living memory, it's instructive to reflect on where Menzies' priorities lay.

In desperate times, with the very future of the nation at stake, defending Australia was his first priority. To forestall inflation and maximise the war effort, Menzies even raised the possibility of transferring purchasing power from the people to the government.

Yet, while cognisant of the potential devastation that runaway inflation posed to the whole economy – and dryly aware of the ability of the wealthy to avoid, or even profit, from it – Menzies never lost sight of the threat posed by inflation to people working hard for a modest wage, or raising a family on the income from a small business.

The thrifty and frugal people he understood as the backbone of the nation were the fundamental pivot upon which his thinking moved.

Thrift, like its cousin frugality, is often derided as an old-fashioned virtue.

"Savers are losers", proclaims popular finance author Robert Kiyoski.

But for Menzies, those who saved for a roof over their heads and a home in which to raise their families – the forgotten and unorganised middle, would form the basis of his new party because they formed the foundation of Australian society.

The historical differentiators usually chime in at this point by pointing out that the people Menzies were addressing were stuck in the middle of a World War.

Many listening around the wireless had lived through the Great Depression, its scarifying impact creating a lifelong predilection for scrimping and saving, only reinforced by wartime rationing.

And yet, today even a cursory look over the popular magazines and the Mum and Dad blogs sprouting over the Internet will find tips for saving, for re-using, for reducing waste and for recycling.

Often blended with environmental aims – and it's surely

conservative to want to conserve resources – these blogs, articles and tweets tap into a deep well of thrift in the Australian psyche.

Despite stagnant incomes and the spiraling cost of electricity, despite bracket creep and creeping duties, levies and taxes from all levels of government, the squeezed middle is continuing to pay down debt and to save.

Thrift is back.

Thrift is helping young people into homes, children into the schools of their parents' choice and older Australians into retirement with dignity.

Thrift buys freedom.

Funds saved through hard work and thrift can be spent at the discretion of the individual on the priorities of the individual.

Freedom to save means freedom to spend, and freedom to invest.

And when individuals exercise that freedom it generates wealth, wisdom and prosperity for our country.

Without that insight, and without that moral understanding, it is easy to inhabit the mindset that governments should shape saving and spending.

Australians, we are regularly told by those who think they know best, save too little – or too much; we spend it on the 'wrong' things or we save using the 'wrong' vehicles.

Of course there will always be the apostles of big finance, earnest and ready to part our savings from the clutches of their competitors.

So long as they are honest in spruiking their wares, the wary saver can judge for themselves which product suits them best.

But the modern Liberal, mindful of Menzies' insight, should always be skeptical of those businesses who seek to enjoin the might of government to 'better manage' our savings or to 'nudge' our thrift in a direction that better suits the policy fashion of the day.

Whenever government usurps thrift through poor economic management, high taxes, or both (and they usually go together, then as now) it strikes at the foundation of national life.

From Menzies to today, the great Liberal insight is that the thrifty are best protected by lowering taxes and managing the economy in a prudent and predictable fashion.

None of this is to deride those who, through no fault of their own, find themselves reliant on the welfare of the state.

But it is to acknowledge that the sustainability of that welfare state depends on those who work and save, and that there is a limit to their capacity to contribute to the national purse without bringing the whole national project undone.

As Menzies perused the newspapers on the day of the broadcast, as usual he would have read the casualty lists, that terrible detail of the dead, the wounded and the prisoners of war – a daily reminder of the nation's suffering and sacrifice.

But his eye must also have been drawn to Prime Minister Curtin's call for austerity, and the response by Fred Stacey, a United Australia Party MP, in the House of Representatives.

Stacey had regaled the House with the story of a Minister who took a petrol-driven car to Melbourne, brought his wife and family back, travelled all round Canberra, and took his wife and family back to Melbourne in the car, which then returned to Canberra.

How, Stacey demanded, could the Government ask people to economise when its own spending was so lax?

Australia is no longer at war, and the demands on the Budget are not as grave, although they still exceed revenue by some margin.

Today's thrifty Australians, labouring under record house prices and a rising cost of living, can reasonably ask their Government to apply the same pressure to its spending that they apply to their own – to practise thrift and reduce waste, to avoid new spending and to live within its means.

22
COMPULSORY UNIONISM

Michaelia Cash

In August 1942, Robert Menzies observed that while trade unions had been a "splendid servant" of the wage-earner, they now "aspire to be a master". Noting unions have "given strength to workers" but also have "militant sections" seeking control over industry and politics, Menzies asked: "what sort of a vested interest will the trades union movement become if it has a compelled and universal membership ...?"

In one sense, Menzies need not have worried. Compulsory unionism has never taken hold as an Australian ideal, largely because, in Menzies words, "in our own casual and cheerful fashion, we do believe in liberty." Far from "universal membership", as Australia's economy has grown and diversified, trade union membership has plummeted. Today, just one in seven workers, and less than 10 percent of private sector workers, belong to a union – a huge drop from thirty years ago, when close to half of the workforce belonged to a union.

Paradoxically however, as union membership has nosedived, their wealth and power has grown substantially. In 2015, Australia's 47 unions received revenues of over $900 million, all income-tax exempt. They're now sitting on net assets worth over $1.5 billion. Today's unions are less focussed on winning hearts and minds, than grabbing wallets. They are no longer simple grassroots organisations focussed on workers.

Today's unions have become major multi-million dollar businesses, focussed on accumulating massive profits. These profits are used to bankroll the unions' subsidiary business – a political party led by a former union leader. In 2015-16 alone, unions donated over $10 million to our political opponents and spent $16 million more on political campaigns against the Government.

While unions now only represent a small fraction of the workforce, their leaders have disproportionate wealth and power. They rail against the "big end of town" but in truth, they are the big end of town. In pursuing their agenda, our opponents and their union masters have in recent times shown callous indifference to those that aren't politically organised. At the same time, we have been reminded of the enduring relevance of Menzies' mission for Liberals: to fight for the Forgotten People.

In early 2016, I started receiving calls from distressed truck drivers, pleading for help. Their livelihoods were being threatened and lives turned upside down, because of a decision by a body called the Road Safety Remuneration Tribunal, established by Bill Shorten as Workplace Relations Minister in 2012. This Tribunal had nothing to do with safety – it was a brutal power grab for the Transport Workers Union at the expense of Australia's 35,000 self-employed truck drivers.

The Tribunal had issued a Payments Order, dictating so called "safe rates" that applied only to owner drivers, discriminating against small family businesses, often in regional Australia. It would have meant for example, if a livestock carrier picked up a partial load from multiple farmers, they would have to charge each farmer the prescribed full rates, as if for a full load. This prescriptive approach doesn't work in a diverse industry. It was intended to force owner drivers to join a big union and drive for a big company, or not drive at all.

To the Coalition Government, these owner-drivers were

Menzies' quintessential Forgotten People, doing their best to go about their business and provide for their families. For our political opponents, these were *Expendable People*. To the relief of these owner-drivers, we secured Senate support to abolish Mr Shorten's Tribunal and in the process, save their livelihoods.

Shortly after this sorry episode, we saw a similar political power grab threatening 60,000 volunteer firefighters in Victoria's Country Fire Authority. The Victorian Government tried to ram through an enterprise agreement containing clauses described by a former Police and Emergency Services Minister in the Bracks Government as "trojan horses" to "side-line CFA volunteers", handing their management to the United Firefighters Union.

This deal meant union interference with the CFA's chain of command, union veto over the CFA's internal policies and union control of community education. It even required volunteer firefighters to wear different uniforms to union firefighters. Despite this having huge implications for volunteers, they had no say. For the sake of a deal, they were cast aside. Fortunately, in October 2016, the Coalition Government successfully amended the Fair Work Act, to protect the operations of emergency services volunteer bodies.

At the end of 2016, the Government secured Senate support for reforms to the building industry, including restoration of the Australian Building and Construction Commission. At one level, these reforms are about productivity in Australia's second biggest industry. They are helping to address the high rate of industrial disputes in construction – which has been around five times the economy average – estimated to add around 30% to the cost of schools, hospitals and other vital infrastructure. At another level, our reforms are about hardworking, law abiding people whose livelihoods and industry have been sabotaged by militant construction unions like the CFMEU.

In recent years, at any given time, there have been around 100 representatives of the CFMEU before the courts, which have imposed over $13 million in fines on the CFMEU and its officials. This clearly hasn't deterred this cashed up, militant union. According to them – and ACTU Secretary, Sally McManus – law breaking is acceptable if you don't like a particular law. They ignore the fact laws are there to protect people and our new laws will protect 1.2 million construction workers who need a cooperative and productive work environment and around 360,000 small businesses in this industry, which rely on a fair system.

The recent campaign against the Fair Work Commission's decision to modify penalty rates highlights the hollow hypocrisy of today's union leaders and how a cosy relationship with big businesses serves to marginalise the "little guy". For years, big unions have done deals with big businesses to pay lower Sunday rates through enterprise agreements. Small businesses however, don't realistically have this option. This means for example, to hire permanent staff on Sundays: a suburban greengrocer has needed to pay $5 an hour more than a major supermarket chain; a family-owned takeaway $8 more than a multinational fast food chain; and a bed and breakfast $10 an hour more than a five-star hotel.

The Commission decided to modify award penalty rates, after hearing extensive evidence from many small businesses – like shop and hotel owners who work on Sundays for free, but would prefer to hire staff and pharmacies that are closed on Sunday, but with moderate changes would provide primary health care seven days a week. It's rare these small business voices are heard in national debates, but they represent a silent majority of employers in this country. We Liberals must stand up for them.

Despite the decline in union membership, trade unions continue to have a legitimate role. They must however be transparent, accountable and abide by the law. To protect the workers who belong to unions, in late 2016 we established a *Registered Organisations Commission*, which requires unions and employer groups to be more transparent and accountable, similar to companies.

Our *Ensuring Integrity Bill* is designed to make it possible for the Federal Court to ban officials from holding office or deregister unions if they continually break the law. It will also apply a public-interest test for union mergers in which a record of lawlessness must be considered. If a company director breaks the law they can be banned and if a driver repeatedly breaks the road rules, they can lose their licence. These community standards should similarly apply to unions.

To further protect honest union members, we're protecting their money. Our *Corrupting Benefits Bill*, which, despite vehement opposition from our opponents, passed the Senate in 2017, bans secret and corrupting payments between employers and unions and requires proper disclosure of legitimate payments. This will tackle the dodgy payments to boost union coffers, membership and political influence, payments to buy industrial peace, or payments for personal gain by union officials.

Our *Proper Use of Worker Benefits Bill* will require proper governance and disclosure of worker benefit funds established to cover redundancies, sickness or other worker benefits. It's unbelievable these basically ungoverned funds could have around $25 million of payments skimmed by unions each year. Workers' funds should be for workers, not piggy banks for union bosses.

At every turn, our political opponents have opposed our efforts to ensure unions act in workers' interest, not their own self-interest. Our opponents' interests apparently lie in protecting cosy arrangements which in turn fund their political machine.

Union leaders have made their intentions clear. If our opponents win the next election, increasingly militant unions will demand significantly more power to strike. They will demand more power to run businesses and industries and more deals to further entrench their wealth and power. The law breakers will become law makers, at the expense of honest workers, small businesses, taxpayers and our economy.

We must not let them. We must continue to fight for the Forgotten People.

23
The Function of the Opposition in Parliament

Christopher Pyne

What is the Function of the Opposition?

It has often been said that even the very best day in opposition is not as good as the worst day in government. Having now served as the Manager of Opposition Business in the House of Representatives and the Leader of the House, I am completely certain of that maxim.

In the 45th Parliament, the Turnbull Government exercises a majority of one in the House of Representatives: the closest majority of any modern Parliament. While I assiduously attend to my duties as the Member for Sturt and the Minister for Defence Industry, my position in the Parliament as the Leader of the House places me at the gap in the fence – the spot where the government and the opposition meet to ensure that the Parliament spends all of its time dealing with the issues that truly matter to Australians.

This is not to say that the Parliament is the 'demilitarised zone' of Australian politics, it is quite the opposite. Parliament is that place that the fiercest disagreements ought to take place but it is also the place that solutions to the biggest problems need to be reached. Solutions can only be reached when an Opposition is willing to fulfil its duty to fearlessly debate the big issues but also to act in the best interest of Australians.

It is incumbent on parliamentarians of all parties and persuasions to keep at the front of our minds that parliamentarians are not the masters of people, but their servants. In opposition it is sometimes easy to lose sight of that because in opposition one has no direct ability to deliver policy results. But that does not diminish the capacity to serve our constituents.

While members of the Executive and government backbenchers can directly implement policies that will make a positive difference in the lives of those we serve, as a member of the Opposition it is easy to feel that your efforts in the Parliament aren't worth very much and very easy to fall in to the supreme trap of opposition for its own sake.

'Playing Politics' versus Joint Responsibility for Unpopular but Necessary Measures

Opposition for its own sake is not parliamentary debate. This is especially true in a modern era where the proliferation of media channels and ease of communication means that a speech in the House is not a Member's only avenue for raising the concerns of their constituents.

The Leader of the House often has the unfortunate duty of 'gagging' debate in the House of Representatives when a certain Bill has been debated for a number of hours and is needed by the Senate. As the munificent Leader of the House that I strive to be, the gag is not exercised lightly or frequently in the 45th Parliament. It is very easy to exercise however when the current opposition rolls out Member after Member to repeat the talking points generated by the Leader's office. Joint responsibility for unpopular but necessary measures, particularly on the issue of budget repair, has not been the strong point of the current opposition.

I would be more than happy to let debate run for days on Bills of critical importance if the Opposition were prepared to approach crucial issues with fidelity to their previously stated policy positions.

Please don't think I am under any illusion that I come to

this subject of the function of an opposition in Parliament with completely clean hands. As Manager of Opposition Business in the 43rd Parliament, I wear my share of the opprobrium that arose from Julia Gillard and Kevin Rudd's Hung Parliament. The Liberal and National Parties were of course focussed on the biggest issues facing Australians but we too were drawn in to the then government's obsession with its own internal rivalries.

That is not to say that nothing of consequence was achieved in the 43rd Parliament. The National Disability Insurance Scheme is a critical piece of social policy that represents the best of Australia. It enjoyed the bipartisan support of the major parties and I hope it will continue to do so into the future as the Turnbull Government implements measures to ensure that it is appropriately funded and managed.

The 43rd Parliament should serve as both a cautionary tale that internal rivalries of political parties only detract from the proper functioning of a Parliament and an example that great social progress can be made when Parliamentarians recognise nation building projects for what they are and work together to legislate for their enduring success.

Conclusion

In 1790 Edmund Burke wrote that society "is a partnership in all science, a partnership in all art, a partnership in every virtue and in all perfection. As the ends of such a partnership cannot be obtained in many generations, it becomes a partnership not only between those who are living, but between those who are living, those who are dead, and those who are to be born."

While the people within our nation's parliament come and go, it is the enduring institution that has woven our country together since the first day of Federation. As such, the Parliament has an obligation not just to the present but to the future.

Menzies understood this when he informed the House of Representatives of the Declaration of War against Nazi Germany. On that day in September 1939, Menzies put not just the case against Hitler, but also the case for parliamentary freedom and debate. He said:

> However long this conflict may last, I do not seek a muzzled Opposition. Our institutions of parliament, and of liberal thought, free speech, and free criticism, must go on. It would be a tragedy if we found that we had fought for freedom and fair play and the value of the individual human soul, and won the war only to lose the things we were fighting for. Consequently I shall welcome criticism, but I do want to emphasise that our great task, however long this struggle may endure, is in common. If we remember that, all criticism will find its right place and its true perspective.

Despite the dangers that were before us, Menzies' reminded the nation of a truth: in a liberal democracy, the Parliament's function is to give expression to the contending opinions which exist in the community. Some of those opinions will, of course, be in opposition to some of the Government's policies. Nevertheless, as members of Parliament, our struggle for Australia is 'in common'. As such, the Opposition has perhaps almost a greater role than the Government in supporting great and brave endeavours that will truly improve the lives of all Australians

24
THE OPPOSITION'S DUTY

Scott Ryan

In crude political terms, the first duty of the opposition is to end its time there and seize the Treasury benches. This is a reasonable perspective for those active in politics. Randolph Churchill's summary was even more simple: the duty of an opposition is to oppose.

The genius of parliamentary democracy was to create the Loyal Opposition, incorporating debate within the constitution and system of government, preventing the exclusion of alternative views through the accusation that difference and debate was disloyalty. This necessarily leads to an expanded role, the promulgation of an alternative as well as commentary on the program of a government.

Opposition is now more potent in Australia than in the Mother of Parliaments, primarily due to our constitutional arrangements. In particular, the powers and role of the Senate provide a forum for an opposition to do more than simply oppose. An opposition can block, frustrate, amend and propose, and occasionally even improve the government through these powers.

Through the nature of our Parliament, an Opposition has more institutional mechanisms to debate and develop an alternative, and even give it legislative form. This is an intrinsic part of Australia's parliamentary democracy. This places an additional responsibility on an opposition in Australia, as it has a greater hand in government than in many comparable parliaments.

To be successful, an opposition must develop and prosecute

an alternative course, one that appeals to the electorate in order to achieve electoral victory, but also provide the basis for a successful period in office. This is its second and equally important duty.

To meet these two objectives, opposition must be selective and positive. Electoral victory alone is not sufficient for an opposition to be successful or to fulfil its duty. It must provide a platform for government, having developed an agenda, the electoral support for it and the processes to underpin its implementation.

In working to deliver these objectives, a modern opposition needs to be cognisant of how our polity has changed in recent decades. Our understanding of community is much less defined by concepts like geography or faith, and how we interact with others has radically changed through the addition of mass electronic form. Consequently, the expectations of citizens about access to information and key public figures is much higher.

In the second decade of this century, the environment in which political parties and members of parliament operate has changed immensely. The impact of new media and the whittling away of mass communication will likely be seen in future years as having as revolutionary an impact as the introduction of television – but with the opposite effect of fracturing audiences rather than providing a common or shared experience.

This increases the importance of this role of an opposition developing a program, for the opportunity to do so when facing the relentless pressures of media and increasing demands from factionalised social groupings when in office is increasingly difficult.

Doing this requires a balance between the priorities of party and political activists and those of the community.

Not only do citizens judge a government according to the times, they judge it according to the quality and consistency of the government's own performance.

In the late 1940s, citizens wanted to maintain new social welfare measures that had been introduced or expanded following depression and a second devastating war, but to draw limits around their expansion. Security was a recurring theme, not just with respect to defence, but for home and economic life. There was a role for government in assisting with this just as there was in limiting government threatening it through the nationalisation of assets and industry, or failing to address industrial lawlessness. In the 1990s, health insurance through Medicare was settled, but there remained strong support for a balanced system that supported private insurance. In both cases, successful oppositions accepted these new settlements but challenged assertions by governments that to query, or to propose balance, limit or alter them reflected a lack of commitment to them. These examples remind us that oppositions must be selective in terms of policies opposed, and occasionally accept new public expectations even if they are proposed by one's opponents. Accepting that certain policy measures have been settled is a key element in addressing the current concerns of citizens, and thereby delivering electoral success, rather than constantly fighting past battles that are sometimes more in the interests of activists than citizens.

Ensuring that time and resources are spend developing and presenting a coherent policy agenda, based on the consistent application of a set of values that underpin priorities ensures the opposition isn't seen as purely opportunistic. As Menzies pithily responded to a critique that he was failing to criticise the government sufficiently, to do so would make him a successful opposition leader, and ensure he remained in that position for many years.

Opposition provides a much greater opportunity for the development of priorities than in government. When considering ideas as opposed to legislation, priorities as opposed to actual budgets, there is not the same need for secrecy, both from the wider public but also from colleagues and other members, that cabinet and cabinet committees require. This is critical not only in testing ideas for feasibility and political potency or acceptability, but also in generating consent for them, both inside a party and in the wider community. An opposition that debates ideas provides an important signal that wider groups have had an opportunity to contribute, building stronger legitimacy into the outcome. To fail to openly debate priorities or measures, particularly when challenging a significant part of a government's agenda, can be seen as acquiescence.

While the media often mistake division for debate, this cannot be allowed to prevent discussion and debate. The new media cycle has empowered vested interests hiding claims under untested claims of the common good. The notion of 'control' of the political agenda and an unexpected announcement generating support is much weaker than decades ago. The temptation of control is a fallacy that limits debate and genuine testing of ideas, which then ensures there is less support for a measure, particularly within a party, but also across the wider community.

With the complexity of policy and range of Commonwealth activity having so dramatically expanded over two decades, combined with the fragmented media environment, more citizens take their cue from disparate sources and groups.

This openness to debate is also critical to determining the priorities of opposition and, hopefully following that period, government. Compounding this is the serious but oft-forgotten fact that governments spend a great deal of effort simply responding to Macmillan's likely apocryphal summary of "events, dear boy, events" well outside their control. No Government can successfully simultaneously tackle all its priorities with equal vigour. So prioritisation is critical both in determining a political agenda and how a government is politically challenged, but also in coming into government as citizens look to priorities to measure values. Absent sufficient specifics, the accusation of breach of faith is levelled almost immediately, and in the modern media era much harder to rebut.

Events also profoundly change the expectations and circumstances of the electorate. New circumstances alter the priorities that citizens have and challenges they expect governments and oppositions to address. Whether it was the 1991 recession 'we had to have' or the global banking crisis of 2008, oppositions make a mistake sticking to a specific policy agenda without reconsidering new circumstances. This is not a justification for inconsistency, as this refers to specific policies, not values that underpin an agenda. The values underpinning the John Howard victory of 1996 and the successful period in government that followed have a direct lineage to those of 1949, even though social, economic and international circumstances were radically different.

Consistency in values does not mean rigid adherence to dogma during changing times. It means, using your values as a guiding point during changing times. For example, the Howard Government consistently argued for a balanced Budget over the economic cycle. This meant that Australia built up surpluses that could be deployed against a potential economic crisis. The ability of Australia to withstand the global economic crisis of 2008 and the Asian Financial Crisis a decade earlier was a direct consequence of prudent budget management by the Howard Government.

Values are a proxy for citizens to assess an opposition. Very few will read specific policy proposals or a policy manifesto. But values and principles illustrated by measures that appeal to certain constituencies and that address specific problems generate consent.

Prosecuting a policy agenda based on key values that are well developed by critiquing a government and proposing alternatives provides predictability, coherence and stability. These are fundamental qualities needed by an opposition seeking to secure support for a change of government and the agenda it seeks to implement. Oppositions that solely seek victory and then articulate and implement a policy agenda following an election will fail though not having generated the support or even consent for their agenda.

As some forces in politics seek to divide Australians, in the past through a flawed construction of class, and in the present, increasingly by issues of identity; the appeal to the national interest, to *the common wealth*, is even more critical for an opposition seeking victory and a mandate to govern.

This does place a new, additional burden on the opposition – it does need to better reflect the community it is seeking support from. No longer do all citizens listen simply to a proposal or an idea, they look to those who argue it. This is not an argument for quotas, but it does mean better representation of those settled issues such as the number of women, and a composition better reflecting modern Australia's cultural antecedence. As Menzies specifically attended to the political interests of women, so does a modern opposition need to tend to the interests of a more diverse Australia.

To those who would argue that it is the job of an opposition to simply oppose, and to hide an agenda or be a minuscule target that attracts no criticism, the public will see through such opportunism.

There is no point winning and then failing to change the country in government.

25
The Government and Ourselves

Tony Smith

At the turn of the last century Australians were the first people anywhere in the world to vote to create a democratic nation.

In the century and seventeen years that have followed, successive generations of Australians have elected 45 Commonwealth parliaments, voting at least every three years.

Almost 515,000 voters elected 75 members of the first House of Representatives. In July 2016 around 14.3 million voters elected the 150 members of the current House of Representatives.

The relationship of voters to the political system and to their elected representatives remains a central issue for the functioning of our democracy. Robert Menzies in 1942, as he gave thought to the post-war world, believed that public debate excessively emphasised the "rights" of citizens to have government give them benefits – what government "owed" them – and gave too little consideration to the real character of a democracy, which was a great joint effort of mutual co-operation and obligation. An almost exclusive focus on rights to government benefits only made sense if you believed that democratic government was something separate from its citizens.

The idea that democracy still derives its vitality from the belief that we "are all in this together", that it is a vast co-operative effort in which we are all partners, and as partners must expect to play our part and to respect our citizen colleagues, and not to expect the worst from them, is perhaps less heard yet remains a key to democracy's success.

Only a tiny minority of communities have ever had the right to choose their own government. In a world of nearly 200 countries, only a minority even today are fully functioning democracies. Through elections, free association, the right to form political groups and parties, a free press, public debate and freedom of speech, we in Australia are all participants in the democratic process. Our representatives, and the governments they form, speak and act on our behalf, and the democratic process ensures that if we do not like what they do, we can dismiss them and choose others to govern us.

What are citizens entitled to expect of their representatives and governments? Certainly not that they will always take wise and good decisions. That would imply they were more than human. But they are entitled to expect that a democratically elected government will respect and defend the basic rights of citizens, that it will listen and respond to legitimate demands, that it will attempt to act in accordance with the best policy principles, and that in all the difficult and complex issues they face, members of parliament will act according to their best judgement of what is in the interests of the people and the country.

A member of Parliament must resist the temptation to choose short term political ends ahead of the national interest. A member of Parliament must be prepared to lead public opinion rather than merely reflect it or, worse, blindly follow it.

Edmund Burke summed this up best in his 1774 speech to the electors of Bristol when, considering the role of Members of Parliament in relation to their constituents: "Your Representative owes you, not his industry only, but his judgement; and he betrays, instead of serving you, if he sacrifices it to your opinion."

Democracy confers heavy responsibilities on the representatives of the people.

But Menzies argued in *The Forgotten People* that democracy also implies responsibilities upon electors themselves beyond simply casting their vote.

Democracy is much more than a mere electoral transaction at the the ballot box, and it is more than simply delivering a government of the people and for the people.

At its best, democratic government relies on constant civic responsibility and engagement by the people for the people. A democracy functions at its best when it is a system of self-government that empowers people to live their lives according to their values, not merely to elect a change of government.

Our participation in the democratic process not only recognises our equal rights to choose a government that represents us, but these rights are matched by obligations to do our duty as citizens: to take part; to help to identify as individuals, and through organisations and groups, the problems we want government to solve; to obey the law; to pay our taxes; to respect our fellow citizens and to be loyal to the nation whose integrity alone makes democracy possible.

In this age of big government, when government agencies attempt to regulate almost every economic and social institution, impacting on the daily lives of citizens as never before, the risk of government being seen as utterly distinct from citizens is vastly increased. As Menzies said, this view undermines the basic spirit on which democracy must be based.

If government is too big, people feel they cannot influence or control it.

One of the key tenets of Liberalism is that government is created to help people live their lives, not to live their lives for them. As John Howard said to the Menzies Research Centre:

A proper balance must be struck between a healthy scepticism about what governments can achieve, and the Australian tradition of believing that there is a role for government which goes beyond it being a mere keeper of the ring. Australians may not want government out of their lives, but they do want it off their backs.

In 1901, Australians voted to elect a federal parliament to help them live their lives; not to abdicate their lives to it. Not only does this limited government protect important freedoms, it has a practical aspect as well. At its essence it recognises that governments are good and indeed very good at some things, but not all things.

If Menzies was right, as I believe he was, to emphasise that the basis of democracy is the idea that "our democracy is all of us", then excessively large and intrusive government threatens that idea.

The idea of limited government embodies a fundamental respect for citizens to live their own lives. As government seeks to control people's lives, it can create a feeling of powerlessness.

At a philosophical level, Liberalism is anchored on this fundamental precept of limited government within the democratic compact between the elector and the elected. A government should be large enough to deliver what individuals and community cannot, but small enough to preserve and protect the vital freedoms which embody the message of self-government: that the privilege of being citizens in a democracy must be based on respect for others and their equal rights and obligations with ourselves.

26
SEA POWER

Cam Hawker

In the years following the Second World War Churchill confided that the only thing that had ever really frightened him during the conflict was the "U-boat peril". Under the command of Eric Raeder, the German Fleet attempted to starve Britain into submission by cutting off vital supplies from America.

The battle of the Atlantic was at its height in 1942 when Menzies spoke on the importance of Sea Power. He was, of course, immediately concerned about Sea Power in the context of the war, and correctly identified that command of the sea was vital if Britain was to prevail against Germany. He also knew it was key to the United States effectively using Australia as base from which to fight Japan.

When Menzies spoke to Australia over the radio on Sea Power, the battles of the Coral Sea and Midway were very recent events, as was the fall of Singapore. This was a period of unprecedented threat for Australia. The war was far from over. However, Menzies also had an eye firmly on the future, and the building of a post-war world. He was convinced that mastery of the seas would continue to be imperative to the balance of power in the world.

To read Menzies on Sea Power is to read his love of history. He evokes the names of the great British seafarers Drake and Nelson. He also speaks of Cook, as he correctly attributes the birth of modern Australia to the might of British Sea Power. However, for Menzies Sea Power was about more than history and the romance of the sea. He knew that for Australia, a country dependant on trade, friendly seas were an economic necessity.

Menzies defined Sea Power as "strength in both naval and merchant shipping." He argued that it is "as an essential ingredient in any modern fleet a large provision of aircraft carriers and of naval aircraft, since it is abundantly plain that large ships without spotting and bombing and fighting aircraft would be as great an anomaly as large ships without long-range guns."

This places Menzies in a debate that consumes Australian defence planners to this day. One group advocates Sea Control, the ability to project power across the high seas to hostile shores, and in doing so secure merchant sea-lanes. Sea Denial is more limited in its ambitions. It seeks to deny the enemy access to one's own home waters by raising the costs of incursion to an unacceptable level. It is more often practised as asymmetric warfare by a weaker power.

Menzies' 1942 remarks locate him firmly as an advocate of Sea Control. Like the great Sea Power theorist Alfred Thayer Mahan, Menzies believed that national greatness was linked with the sea, the ability to control it in war and to maximise its commercial use during peacetime. Though I would argue that we should not concern ourselves too much with the specific approach to naval strategy Menzies took when we read him today. The salient points are that Menzies recognised the role of Sea Power in determining the course of both the war and the peace that was to come after it and that he knew it had a special relevance for the island continent.

Menzies knew that for Australia, a country with a small population and vast landmass, that is geographically isolated, Sea Control is only possible in concert with the forces of 'great and powerful friends'. This was of course the policy of the war, when the Americans came to utilise Australia as a great unsinkable aircraft carrier. However, this approach also informed post-war policy. This thinking motivated Menzies' Minister for External Affairs, Percy Spender's pursuit of a 'Pacific Pact' and the signing of the ANZUS Treaty. The policy of Forward Defence, which saw Australia take an active role in supporting British and American operations in South East Asia, became central to the Menzies' Government of the 1950s and 60s. It was borne of the judgment Australia's security was best preserved by engaging with allies to counter threats far from home least they spread to our own shores.

It may seem strange to us that as long ago as 1942, Menzies felt the need to defend the continued importance of Sea Power in the face of emergent technology around Air Power. We see a similar dynamic today. With the spread of the internet, globalisation of capital and great advances in technology, it is easy to forget that shipping remains vital to the global economy, and for no country more so than Australia. Today we talk of the importance of securing 'sea lines of communication' through dominance of the 'global commons' that is the world's oceans.

In Menzies' youth, the British Empire was maintained by the Royal Navy's ability to control those global commons. Today, the US Navy remains the world's only true blue-water navy with the ability to project force without contest around the world thanks to its carrier battle groups. This unique power is now in question for the first time since 1945 as China develops its Anti-Access or Sea Denial capability.

On returning to the prime ministership in 1949, Menzies inherited a Royal Australian Navy (RAN) already scaled back after its wartime service. He went on to significantly expand those capabilities, particularly in the second half of his tenure. This included the development of a naval aviation capability, and the expansion and modernisation of the RAN's submarine service, with the acquisition of *Oberon Class* submarines. The purchase of the American *Adams Class* guided missile destroyer, designated the *Perth Class* destroyer in its RAN service, was a significant step in the development of our navy. Although reforms would continue well into the 1970s and beyond, much of the basic structure of today's fleet would be familiar to Menzies.

When we read Menzies on Sea Power today, our thoughts naturally turn to the power shifts in our own region. The re-emergence of China as a great power and its challenge to an American primacy that has served us extremely well. More specifically our thoughts are likely to turn to the challenge posed by Beijing's assertive stance in the South China Sea, a challenge that we have correctly read in the context of the control of the global commons and freedom of navigation.

As Liberals, it is perhaps tempting to ask ourselves what would Menzies do? In the same way that American evangelicals might ask what Jesus would do. It is an impulse probably best ignored in terms of prescriptive answers, but we can look to Menzies' history and approach to the challenges of his own premiership for broader guidance. It is a safe bet to assume that Menzies would be a supporter of the recent and ongoing modernisation of the RAN, which includes upgrades or outright replacement of both the surface and submarine fleets.

It is likely that Menzies would see the political capital to be had in the renewed empathies on the importance of a local defence industry, including a ship building industry. Although his own history of defence procurement suggests that he was certainly not adverse to be budgetary benefits of buying kit off the shelf.

It is reasonable to assume that Menzies would broadly agree with the concept of a navy that operates closely with those of our allies. However, it likely he would also argue for a core self-reliant capability, and the ability to conduct independent operations. Some aspects of Sea Power today may cause Menzies regret, the decline of Australia's merchant fleet and foreign ownership of some of our ports come to mind.

We can be sure in assuming that Menzies would seek to meet the challenge of a re-emerging China in the familiar context of the US alliance and that he would regard Sea Power as vital to this. What would he make of the current president? He would likely be appalled, but just as likely he would see the need to maintain the alliance because it continues to in Australia's interests. Though it is important to add that he would seek to navigate it in a way that was consistent with those interests.

Menzies' rhetoric on the alliance speaks much of the shared values and common history of two English-speaking peoples. This was important to him. Yet, Menzies was also a pragmatist. As a pragmatist, he knew that Australian and American interest coincide often but not always. Pragmatism caused Menzies to accept that recognising the People's Republic of China risked alienating the US in a difficult climate, while allowing him to see that it was prudent to maintain a trade relationship in non-strategic goods with Beijing, despite Washington's misgivings.

During the first Taiwan Straits Crisis in 1954-55, Menzies took a principled yet pragmatic position in defining to Washington exactly how he saw Canberra's obligations under ANZUS in relation to a conflict over offshore islands held by the Nationalists. Menzies also engaged in consultative diplomacy with mutual allies to urge the US to adopt a measured policy in response to Beijing's provocations. This arguably helped prevent a local crisis lapsing into a broader war. It certainly strengthened Menzies' reputation as a statesman.

For Menzies Sea Power was linked to Australia's national interests in terms of both economic and strategic security. He was also highly conscious of its importance to the existence of what he might have called the 'free world', no abstract concept in 1942, or indeed in the Cold War which dominated his second premiership.

For Menzies, who spoke of 'great and powerful friends' in the plural, the ANZUS alliance was part of the broader Western Alliance. Menzies knew that this alliance was necessary to ensure freedom of navigation and open access to the global commons. That necessity endures. The expansion of the People's Liberation Army – Navy (PLA-N) and development of the Maritime Silk Road Strategy to sit alongside the One Belt One Road Initiative, tell us that Beijing also recognises the importance of Sea Power. However, these developments invite responses based on pragmatism as well as principle. In crafting these, the next generation of policy makers would do well to look to Menzies own diplomatic legacy.

27
THE STATUTE OF WESTMINISTER

Dean Smith

One of the distinguishing characteristics of conservatism is that it is anchored in a thoroughly realistic worldview. Conservatives are not pessimists, as some of their critics are want to assert. However, we are realistic to recognise that, despite our best efforts and intentions, there are occasions when negative things happen.

There are economic downturns, wars, violent crimes, outbursts of civil unrest, natural disasters – and it is a basic tenant of conservative thought that we should not only do everything that is possible to prevent them, but just as importantly, have contingency plans in place in case they do.

It is for this reason that Australian conservatives have spent the past decade arguing that we need to return the Budget to surplus. Of course, we strive to make certain that negative economic events do not occur – but if the worst happens, we want Australia to have a 'buffer' in place to soften the negative effects.

In the same way, we place a strong emphasis on ensuring our defence forces are in the strongest possible position to deal with the conflicts we fervently hope will not arise, and support our emergency services to deal with natural disasters when they occur.

Similarly, the overwhelming majority of Australian conservatives will do everything possible to prevent our nation becoming a republic. Changing the nation's system of government is, almost by definition, a revolutionary act – and conservatives prefer the evolutionary to the revolutionary.

I remain convinced that Australians will never support a move to a republic, and the reason is simple. Despite almost 45 years of advocacy (if we date the birth of 'serious' republicanism from the time of Gough Whitlam's dismissal), its evangelists still cannot point out how anyone's life would be improved, much less our democracy enhanced, were we to make such a change.

Republicans' best arguments (and affixing that appellation to their talking points is an act of the greatest charity) generally revolve around appeals to emotion, rather than reason. They will assert that "our head of state should be one of us", or that "our children should have the right to grow up to be President".

Notwithstanding that fact that our head of state already is "one of us", and I am yet to hear a single child express any desire to occupy such an office, these arguments are hardly a compelling reason to overturn 117 years of remarkable constitutional stability.

There now seems to be a consensus among many republicans that what did them in when Australians last voted on this question in 1999 was not that their arguments were poor, but the model proposed was flawed.

As a result, some of those who argued in 1999 that a republican model permitting the direct election of a President by the people was a dangerous and risky one are now either holding their tongues, or are actively promoting the idea that such a model be submitted to the people.

It should be noted at this point that there are both constitutional monarchists and republicans within the Liberal Party. This must be respected, and people should be free to articulate their point of view and participate in debates about a republic.

Yet, I strongly suspect that even the most fervent republicans within the Liberal Party would hold grave reservations about a republican model which permitted for direct election of Australia's head of state. Yet, it is now entirely possible that the other side of politics will appeal to populist extremes by actively promoting such a model.

Indeed, the current Opposition Leader refuses to rule that out. This is despite the fact that Australia's most prominent republican Paul Keating, clearly highlighted the folly of such a system.

In documents prepared for the Keating Cabinet in the mid-1990s, it was noted that a directly elected President "might be tempted to assume, or presume to take moral authority from a popular national mandate ... and exercise the powers of that office in a manner which could bring the office into competition with the government of the day."

This is why the Keating Government supported a republican model which would see the President elected by two-thirds of the members of the Commonwealth parliament. They could see direct election would establish a rival mandate, and enshrine instability into Australia's constitutional arrangements.

For today's republican movement to ignore this advice demonstrates a lack of maturity, and rank opportunism. Monarchists and republicans alike within the Liberal Party must consider how to respond.

Keating's Cabinet was further warned that this would "fundamentally change the character of Australian Government" and "move our parliamentary democracy towards an executive presidency". In other words, our system would become more like that of the United States of America, with enormous power vested in a single individual for a set number of years.

Of course, America is an enormously important trading and defence ally – but I am yet to meet a single Australian who believes our system of government should more closely mirror theirs.

If a future Government puts the republican question to a basic 'Yes/No' referendum, as is the Opposition's current policy, then the Liberal Party must unite to defeat any attempt to institute a direct election model.

Whatever position individual Liberals may hold on the question of a republic, all of us have an obligation to oppose any further dilution of parliamentary sovereignty, and the concomitant instability it would undoubtedly bring.

Further, as is the case with budget repair, we should not wait until the rainy day arrives before taking action. The time to highlight the dangers of a directly elected head of state is now – not in the wake of a 'Yes' vote on the question of the republican question.

Australian has enjoyed well over a century of constitutional stability almost without peer in the democratic world. It is impossible to overstate the important role the unifying role of the Crown has played in promoting that stability, and not even the most devoted direct-electionist republican can demonstrate how their preferred system could achieve the same ends.

The republicans will say that opposition to direct election means that I don't trust the people. On the contrary, it means I don't trust political parties not to turn the contest into another breach in the partisan divide.

Not even the most enthusiastic supporters of direct election can give a guarantee that the presidency will not become another front in the tiresome 'culture wars'.

Instead of an office of unity, we will have an office of disunity. Instead of choosing a candidate above politics, we will get a president that is the result of politics. Instead of an umpire, we will get another political warrior. Instead of the best of us being called to the office, the best will be repulsed by the negative campaigning and the politics of personality and smear that seem to accompany so many elections. And instead of a head of state who unites us, we will get heads of state who will, in time, become alternate voices to the elected prime minister, and to the parliament itself.

The arguments are on our side – but they will not advance themselves. Accordingly, all Liberals must commit to the protection of parliamentary sovereignty in Australia. It is imperative that we reject any attempt to move towards an all-powerful head of state, directly elected in a process that would entrench partisan politics in our Constitution, and thus undermine its integrity.

28

SCHOOLS AND THE WAR

Ross Fox

Education is the greatest form of national defence. It is the character and initiative of Australia's citizenry that will determine our nation's enduring prosperity or decline more than any military capability we assemble. Australia neglects its schools, technical colleges and universities at its peril. The risk of neglect extends far beyond questions of material resources. Our educational institutions contribute far more than training workers as inputs to the national economic output.

Schools are wondrous time machines of humanity. Every Australian school, vocational education institution and university creates our nation's future one person at a time in the lives their students live out. 'School' should properly be understood as meaning 'Here the future is made'.

Robert Menzies said:

> As a nation we cannot afford to do anything less than our best in a campaign the result of which will be to determine whether, in the new world, we are to be a nation of strong, self-reliant, trained and civilised people, or whether we are to be content with second-rate standards, and more devoted to the pursuits of material advantage than to the achievement of a genuine humane community spirit.

This is no truer than in our nation's schools.

Whatever the risk of material neglect of technical colleges, universities and schools a graver risk for Australia lies in the purpose of education growing into a melange of relativism and falling subservient to an instrumental end.

Drawing on his experience as a teacher Pope Francis has said "Education cannot be neutral. It is either positive or negative; either it enriches or it impoverishes; either it enables a person to grow or it lessens, even corrupts him. The mission of schools is to develop a sense of truth, of what is good and beautiful. And this occurs through a rich path made up of many ingredients. This is why there are so many subjects — because development is the result of different elements that act together and stimulate intelligence, knowledge, the emotions, the body, and so on."

An education worth its name must be about values and the needs of the whole person as a person rather than merely a future worker.

Australia is a genuinely exceptional nation in respect of our school education system. The scope, diversity and quality of government, Catholic and independent schools is a credit to the national vision. Two momentous movements have nurtured the jewel we treasure today.

In the latter half of the 19th century the separate colonies of Australia passed Education Acts. Foremost among the innovations contained therein was the enshrining of the settlement of compulsory, free and secular school education provided by the then colonial governments. A century later Menzies recognised the right of parents to choose how their children would be educated by advancing government support for non-government schools, largely Church schools, in the form of state-aid.

As the Minister for Education, Senator Simon Birmingham explained in his speech to Catholic educators from across Australia in June 2016: "It was the Coalition under Prime Minister Robert Menzies who listened to your leaders, understood the issues facing the sector, and in an atmosphere of co-operation and trust, put aside any ideological and personal religious beliefs, and started funding the Catholic and non-government sector. That support grew and was developed on the principles of government making a contribution to every student's education, ensuring parents can exercise choice, respect for different religious views, meeting need, encouraging diversity and understanding that for some, education does not just have a secular purpose."

Although colonial education acts of the 1800s established compulsory, free and secular government schools in the main schools were not absent religious influence. Secular did not denote non-belief and school systems facilitated ongoing direct engagement with scriptural and religious instructors making provision within school time for local religious ministers to teach children. This convention continues today.

A common and simple definition of secular is "not connected with religious or spiritual matters". Enshrining government schools as secular in the 1800s did not mean they were free from religion and certainly not anti-religious.

In recent years the place of Christmas carols in government schools has been questioned and new policies issued to assist school leaders navigate this apparently challenging issue. 'Secular' was historically observed as pluralist and inclusive of diversity in faith and religion. As even Christmas carols are questioned it could now have morphed to be interpreted as atheistic or anti-religion.

The purpose of schooling in Australia was agreed and jointly proclaimed by all state, territory and commonwealth Education Ministers in the *Melbourne Declaration on Educational Goals for Young Australians* in December 2008. According to the *Declaration*: "Schools play a vital role in promoting the intellectual, physical, social, emotional, moral, spiritual and aesthetic development and wellbeing of young Australians, and in ensuring the nation's ongoing economic prosperity and social cohesion."

If education is a holistic endeavour for the child it cannot be truly secular. It cannot neglect the reality of the spiritual dimension of individuals however they choose to express this spirituality.

An 'education' is manifestly inadequate if it is limited to the transmission of 'secular' knowledge. What society needs to arise from the encounter of the child and their learning about themselves and the world is more than for them to learn by rote certain facts, relationships and truths. An education worthy of Australian children and our nation's future cannot be limited to the secular.

The recent affliction of 'fake news' conceived by citizen journalists and spread by social media may not be an enduring phenomenon. The ability to spread mistruths so easily with apparent credibility is a concern. Arguably the problem would be better addressed if every citizen were armed with an education that imbued them with critical faculties and hence inoculated them against being inveigled by falsehoods. As Menzies said of his desire for an educated polity: "We shall become perfectly democratic only when every citizen is given the spiritual, mental and physical training which he is capable of receiving."

The question 'Who is all this education for?' is presumed too often. School education should not be a statist endeavour to fill empty vessels with the enlightened wisdom of the prevailing regime. In accepting compulsory schooling parents should not cede their parental authority, responsibility and aspiration for the development and flourishing of their child. As school education policy is nationalised encroaching into curriculum, teacher training, registration and recognition, testing and much else besides the risk of further alienating parents in the education of their children looms.

Australia must be wary of uncritically seeking consistency and uniformity across a country as diverse as ours. Drawing all aspects of education to be nationally consistent is unlikely to salve to the ills we face. Montesquieu wrote in the age of enlightenment: "the idea of uniformity appealed to little minds, who found in it a species of perfection". Menzies reflected: "In a continent like ours, with immense varieties of physical and human characteristics, variety should be developed.."

For the good of parents, students and the nation, education cannot be limited to a secular endeavour. Nor should it be one size fits all. Education is too important an endeavour to be denuded of all values by the benevolent and well intentioned bureaucratic apparatus of the state.

Australia holds a precious jewel in the diversity of its education system across government, Catholic and independent schools. Whatever the differences the reality is that each pillar of the educational trinity benefits from the diversity and contribution of the other. This precious jewel was undoubtedly enhanced by the foresight and vision of a leader such as Menzies.

Let us renew our commitment, whether as parents, educators, concerned citizens or life-long learners to an education in every Australian school that is truly worthy of the name.

29
THE MORAL ELEMENT IN TOTAL WAR

Jim Molan

One of the greatest successes of post-World War Two Australia is that most of us have been protected from the consequences of what previous generations knew as total war, or wars of national survival. Ironically, the fact that we have not experienced such war for over 70 years is also one of the biggest difficulties in preparing this nation for the probability of future wars. Many Australians just don't believe that the kind of total war, discussed by Menzies in his broadcast *The Moral Element of Total War* could ever happen again.

But there is still evil in the world and when evil is combined with modern weaponry, the results are horrendous. Industrial age warfare is still with us, and in our recent memory a million died in the Iran-Iraq War, uncountable barbarity is being experienced in parts of Africa, Syria is ten times worse than Iraq ever was, the Middle East exists on a knife edge, China now controls the South China Sea and nuclear armed powers look at each other from behind screens of missiles. Of concern, some of these nuclear players are not the relatively stable nations that allowed civilisation to survive the Cold War.

The US sees the threat to itself and the West through the mantra of "four nations and an ideology". The four nations are a fragile but expansionist Russia, an aggressive and rich Iran, a powerful but resentful China and an unpredictable North Korea, plus of course the ideology we fight every day, Islamic Extremism. This simple prescription of "four countries and an ideology" used by the US to frame the threats in the world leaves out South America, most of Africa, and the potential for conflict in the sub-continent. Since the end of World War Two, the world has not been as unpredictable as it is now, that unpredictability is growing, and much of the potential conflict is in the regions surrounding Australia.

Australians should never think that the era of total war experienced in the two world wars will never be experienced again. Australia is not buying fighters, submarines and ships at an historic rate to deliver humanitarian aid to foreign countries. Australia is modernising its armed forces because there is a deep belief within the defence, security and intelligence community in Australia that war is more than just possible. For a variety of reasons, that belief is not reflected in the community as a whole.

In classifying the domestic terrorism threat, we say it is 'Probable' because there is "both the intent and capability" to conduct terrorist attacks. Even if you put the ongoing nuclear crisis with North Korea to one side, war between states is at least probable, with the probability growing, because at least the above four nations have developed the capability and may have the intent to attack the West. Terrorism will never bring the nation down, but state on state warfare might well do that. Are we as well prepared for state on state war as we are for terrorism?

Defence is not just ships, planes and tanks. It is far more. It is national resolve, resilience and leadership, culture and confidence, diplomacy, generalship and strategy, statesmanship and luck. All of this is the moral element of defence. Only then is defence about weapons.

Australia has changed dramatically since the end of World War II. In both world wars it was seen as the norm that a relatively culturally and racially homogenous Australia would deploy its forces overseas to defend the UK and Europe. Australians were technically British subjects at the time, although within a sovereign country. The institutions that defined our civilisation were British from a Judeo-Christian base and to defend them against fascism and totalitarianism was natural at the time, and may well be natural again in the future.

The multicultural nature of modern Australia may provide a challenge to a unifying moral approach in an extreme situation caused by war. Australia has significant Sub-continent, Chinese and Middle East races within our national make-up. Also the religious affiliations of many Australian citizens cross national boundaries, especially in the case of Islam. The impact of the Irish Catholic (referred to until recently as 'Roman' Catholic) influence in the conscription issue in World War 1 had a dramatic impact on Australian military capacity on the Western Front, and Australian Catholics of Irish heritage were far more culturally compatible with the Australia of that time than is likely to be the case with certain ethnic and religious groups today. The role of Australian citizens of Chinese descent in influencing domestic and international policy on behalf of Chinese interests has been a matter of public concern recently, particularly in relation to the South China Sea. In any extreme situation, divided loyalty will detract from the moral factor in national power.

Political reality means that there will be no going back on the roughly one million Australians who have dual citizenship. But the uncertainty in the world and in our region should encourage government to stress the need from now on, for all who come to live permanently in this country to show allegiance only to Australia. Government should support the importance of the moral element in extreme circumstances by requiring the one and only loyalty of a new citizen is given to Australia, and that is manifest through renunciation of any other citizenship. For good reason our constitution requires that our political leaders do not have "split allegiances". The justification should be exactly the same for every citizen.

The moral element in war, therefore, goes to the need for government to take every step to link Australians into Australian culture and values, critical in an extreme conflict situation. There is a strong tendency in Australia and across many Western countries to downplay the importance of citizenship. Many countries permit dual citizenship, and this was a system that could be tolerated in Australia's case when many of the nations involved (UK, Canada, Ireland, US, New Zealand) were similar. Commentators who do not acknowledge the importance of the moral element in the strength of a nation as expressed in citizenship, are unlikely to acknowledge the importance of allegiance only to Australia.

As citizens of a country that may need to rely on the moral factor in an extreme circumstance, not only must our loyalty be towards this country before any other, but also in exercising our democratic right as voters to vote responsibly in relation to defence. But in modern Australia there is a serious problem in doing this.

The problem I refer to applies to all Australian post-World War II governments: we voters do not have any idea whether we are adequately defended by our government; and we currently have no way of finding that out or of making an assessment against which we can vote. We tend to assume that because we are spending what is a lot of money on defence, we must be well defended. This problem applies not only to the acquisition of weaponry but also to the far more complicated non-military aspects of defence referred to above. It has been shown time and again that a nation can have the best weapons in the world but success in war is about more than just weapons, and if the moral aspect is weak or missing, then the probability of failure is unacceptably high.

The inability to judge the adequacy of our own defence occurs because defence policy over the years is all about inputs to defence and has nothing to do with defence policy outputs. Our defence policies over the years list ships, planes and tanks that are to be acquired, but they are all inputs. Winning wars is the most important defence output, and that is only partially about weapons. Interestingly, not having a coherent defence policy has not really mattered for the last 70 years. Now in current strategic circumstances, it has become critical.

In this new and dangerous strategic environment, governments must be prepared to commit to defence outputs, to being able to win wars, not just commit to having the weapons that are inputs. To do this governments must specify what in their opinion the next war will be like, at least generically, and to state the most dangerous operational scenario that Australia is likely to face, and how the government will confront it.

And governments must be prepared to say this publicly so that we the voters can hold governments accountable for our defence. To claim that a general operational statement of the object of defence policy is classified is just not true. Our specific contingency plans against specific countries or eventualities should be classified, but not the standard to which we should build our defences before a specific threat develops. Ironically, at the moment, every foreign military intelligence analysts whose job it is to study Australia knows more about the ability of the ADF and Australia to win a conflict than Australian citizens will ever know.

The problems for voters is that almost the only thing that we can judge is expenditure – we said we would spend two per cent by 2019 and we achieved that or we did not. But does that equal success? Defence is about winning not spending.

In declaring Australia's support for the US against North Korea in the current crisis, Prime Minister Turnbull reminded us that the US is the central pillar of our defence policy. Just as the US would come to our aid, so the Prime Minister committed Australia to going to the US's aid. This relationship with the US is held by all America's allies, from NATO across the Middle East to Asia.

The US has been central to our defence since the end of World War Two. But following 15 years of war in the Middle East and eight years of Obama's policies and Congress' sequestration, the US has never been less capable of coming to the aid of its allies. For decades the allies, including Australia, have assumed that they could spend comparatively little on defence over the decades because in extremis, the US as the dominant superpower will always come to our rescue. We could afford incoherent defence policies.

This may no longer be true at a time when the US is comparatively weaker (except for its nuclear umbrella) and there are four powers (Russia, Iran, China and North Korea) of considerable strength. As has happened now for years, the ideology of Islamic Extremism complicates all aspects of the strategic environment.

In looking at the moral element as it applies to governments in preparing for war, defence has a claim to being unique in comparison to other government policies. If Australians are unhappy with the health or education policy for example, they can purchase more or different health and education services from the non-government sector, or they can vote against a government that does not deliver the services they want. If Australians are unhappy with defence, they cannot go anywhere else. So government has a moral responsibility to voters that it may not have with any other services such as education and health.

We pay governments to take risk in areas such as NBN, NDIS and Gonski. In each of these we quickly see if the risk is being managed by government. We know when we do not have download speeds, the NDIS budget blows out, or spend Gonski money for no improvement in standards. When is it that we the voter finally sees that defence is inadequate? When the wolf is at the door? By then, given the time it takes to prepare a modern defence force, it is too late.

This has led us into what I call the two per cent trap. We have said for years that the standard in defence expenditure that we need to meet is two per cent. And in Australia's case we are about to meet it. But that was a standard which we failed to meet in the past, that only few NATO countries currently meet, and which was a good figure when the US dominated the world. Then all we had to do to ensure our survival was to send small forces to US wars at irregular intervals.

Well, the US can no longer come to the aid of all its allies. There is not enough US cavalry to come galloping over the hill to scatter the indians. Yet we still strive for two per cent. This is counter intuitive, but government is unlikely to change unless we the voters demand it, or there is a strategic scare. And in modern terms, we are highly unlikely to be afforded years to react to a specific threat. No strategic scare worthy of the name is likely to give us greater than six months to prepare. And of course, if we are preparing for war, then others in the world are also likely to be preparing. There will not be hundreds of JSF available for sale to those who had not prepared.

To achieve the moral element in total war government must take a logical and open output focus on defence so that we the voters can understand the risk that government is taking in our name. You cannot logically express risk by saying that you will have 12 submarines by the 2050s. But you can do so by specifying the most dangerous generic threat that the government is preparing for, to meet that threat we need a defence force of a certain capability in a certain time period, and if we are deficient in a number of capability areas, then specify them. Government should then say that to remedy deficiencies, Australia would need to spend a certain amount of money. Governments would need to tell voters whether they are prepared to spend that amount of money or not, and this represents the risk that government is taking in our name. Voters would then be able to assess that risk.

The moral element in war, total or otherwise, is critical. The moral element can be impacted on adversely if governments do not insist that the first loyalty of every Australian citizen is towards Australia, a loyalty that is manifest by a willingness to renounce all other loyalties and citizenships, especially in preparing for an extreme situation. With the moral element established, voting Australians should ensure that governments acting in the name of voters are not taking excessive risk in relation to the military and non-military aspect of defence, by being prepared to engage its citizens directly and openly on its defence policy.

That this is not occurring can only make one suspicious that there are massive deficiencies in our defences, both military and moral, which government is too embarrassed to be open about.

30

THE LAW AND THE CITIZEN

Natalie Ward

The Liberal Party has had more than its fair share of lawyers. All but one of our Prime Ministers studied the law. The one who didn't John Gorton was a passionate reformer of law which is its own delicious irony.

Our parliamentary ranks, state and federal, have always attracted lawyers. Some like Menzies were eminent in the law before politics, and others like Sir Garfield Barwick, Tom Hughes QC, and John Dowd QC scaled the heights of the law after politics.

But it shouldn't be a surprise that the Liberal Party attracts lawyers, because the law itself is grounded in the liberal traditions of personal and property freedoms, parliamentary representation, access to the law and an independent court system.

The railway tracks of our parliamentary and legal systems are the means by which our country delivers representation, fairness and justice for all citizens. The parliament has the power of legislation based on the authority given to it by the people, and the countervailing power of the law to protect citizens from abuse of power. As Menzies said in 1942, ''The law's greatest benefits are for the minority man – the individual.' And again, 'If the day is to come when the courts are to be closed to the aggrieved citizen ... then that day will cast a black shadow across British freedom.'

Because of this, law and politics have always gone hand in hand. They are like siblings. Law is the first born perfect child – sensible, straight, even boringly compliant. Politics is the younger sibling, in bigger families often the adored youngest, 'the baby', breaking the rules, offending others with its rashness and non-compliance.

And no one understood this better than Menzies, the eminent barrister with an impressive record arguing before the High Court, who chose to forge a second, equally impressive, career in politics. He demonstrated his deep understanding of the connectedness of law and politics when he wrote "Politics proved to be my greatest duty. But the law remained my first love".

Many lawyers, including me, are attracted to politics. Mostly because what attracts us to the law is the intrinsic meaning of the work. It's an uncommon word these days, but the law and politics are both 'vocations'. We participate because we believe in the power of both to right wrongs and deliver a better world. That's hard to say in a world that prefers the cynical, but I know it to be true.

I believe in the law and the role of the Parliament because it calls us to think beyond our election campaigns. It challenges us to consider the current needs of our nation as bounded by our constitution, drafted by our forefathers in thoughtful, progressive, considered and balanced liberal argument.

My passion to serve was first ignited by my parents, and then my desire to change things for the better was honed as my work as a lawyer and political adviser exposed me to the reality of hardships faced by people from many different cultural and social backgrounds. In my one attempt to appeal to the High Court, led by my colleague and husband David Begg, we sought to shine a light on the darkness of childhood sexual abuse. I like to think we played a little part in the movement that delivered a royal commission.

The wrongs and injustices were initially raised in law. Following a rocky road, they are today rectified by amendment to law, by the state and federal parliaments. The irony and beauty of how the two work together, hand in hand, was no more prescient for me than when I sat in the Parliament and was able to speak on legislation for NSW to be the first parliament to implement a National Redress Scheme. Those injustices are just now being rectified (or at least redressed) in politics. On that day, my two careers danced together. Hand in hand. Side by side. The law and politics melded together to find a way forward.

That is not to say I am totally starry eyed about the law or politics or blind to its failings. I am not. At their worst, they reflect human vanity and generate distrust, discord and a loss of human dignity. At their best, they create a better, fairer world. What separates the two is an ethos of service. For me, my purpose is unflinching: I entered politics, *ut prosim*, "that I may serve".

To many people 'the law is an ass', and, in my limited 20 year experience of the law, parties to a dispute are often frustrated by the law and the legal process. And yet, despite its flaws, the law is more important than ever as a stable, clear and unbiased foundation for the determination of rights and obligations.

Guided by principles and tradition, the law can adapt. It is what has helped our societies transition in this tremendous era of iRevolution. Transformations like Uber regulation and recognition that 'the internet of things' is part of our lives has happened because our legal system is responsive to change when it is needed. It may not be immediate, but after considered deliberation, the law can and does, adapt. Equally, when it comes to our freedoms, the law stands as the bulwark to defend citizens from threats to privacy, defamation, and the threats of terror and international espionage.

The Parliament is the people's voice in the law. Like Menzies' time, we are living in an era when Parliamentary democracy is being questioned. As liberals we should take stock and ask how is the law and the Parliament serving the people today?

In my view, there is a huge contrast between the considered arguments of our forefathers and our contemporary fast and furious approach. Much of public life is now communicated through 'grabs and tweets'. The theatre of the Parliament seems to be triumphing over the substance of governing.

Have we have forsaken the opportunity to build thoughtful arguments and the considered case for public policy, in exchange for the quick grab or the easy defence? To the public, the quick fix of modern media has become the quick shag of politics. In so doing, loyalties are not strengthened, values are not underpinned and all of us, feel disappointed in a system of government, when we shouldn't be.

Modern culture treats politics as dysfunction. But we must never forget that debate is healthy. We should test arguments and give a voice to opposing views, because all too often, the maverick of today drives what ultimately becomes commonly accepted change. Indeed, it was the maverick John Gorton who first argued in a parliament in the 1970s for the decriminalisation of homosexuality.

We must challenge the idea that somehow representative politics is dysfunction. It's not. It's the clearing house of ideas that drives change and delivers justice.

For us as Liberals, parliamentary government and the law is a means to an end. It brings certainty.

In a time when many use equality as an argument for change, it is worth recalling that the courts offer citizens that very foundation. The law is beyond class and applies equally to every citizen, from road or parking offences to serious criminal offences to legal challenges to legislation. Indeed, two former members of the Parliamentary chamber that I am a member of now reside in gaol because they did not understand that simple concept. And no surprises, they weren't liberals.

The Law and the Citizen

The law is the arbiter. Like a parent refereeing a squabble between siblings, the law finds a way to bring certainty and justice. Even in the world of politics, where it often seems that the principles of law, fairness, justice, proper process and natural justice do not apply, we can be guided by, soothed by, and sometimes even cling to the law. Like a lifeboat in rough seas, like a compass in the bush, the law is our north, south, east and west. As Menzies said, 'The long-established and noble rule of Law' is "one of the greatest products of the character and tradition of British history ...".

In politics today, sibling states fight with each other over taxes. The division of the GST pie, a prime cause of dispute, was a concept unknown to Menzies. Yet it was very much on his radar as he defended the right of the States to go to the High Court and 'argue the toss' against each other and test Commonwealth legislation. He defended this right even in the face of criticism that the States' action was un-Australian, because it was done during the darkest days of war.

As Menzies so rightly recognised, even in the face of political unpopularity, the slippery slope of subjectively choosing when, and when not, to observe the law is too dangerous to ignore. It must be turned to first and last.

Never was this more prescient on the world stage than today. A 'rules based' international system is under threat. Recently the world witnessed Russia breach the sovereignty of the United Kingdom by poisoning an "enemy" and his daughter.

Acts of lawlessness, even by foreign powers, have no place in countries that believe in the rule of law – and who uphold the rights of citizens to live free and peaceful lives.

Our Prime Minister, Malcom Turnbull, supported international action. He worked with our Commonwealth allies to uphold the law and to say 'No, not on our watch.'

When the rule of law has been broken, we Commonwealth countries work together to protect our respective people. A blight on one is a blight on us all. Laws have been broken, and we will draw a line in the sand to say that this behaviour is not acceptable on the world stage. Like family members who may often furiously squabble, nonetheless when one is threatened, we immediately stand together. For me, that was a seminal moment, when politics and law hold hands via our leaders on the world stage. They stood together to say "No" to a Russian school yard bully.

As we reflect on Menzies' question about the citizen and the law, it can be easy to believe that Menzies points us back to the past. He doesn't. His voice is a principled and pragmatic voice for today. As the Prime Minister said on the 2015 *Howard on Menzies* documentary series, Menzies "would be talking about the realities of 2015 not the realities of 1955".

I agree with Prime Minister Turnbull. The times and the issues of our era are different from Menzies', but liberal values are timeless, and Menzies was always in keeping with the times. He was pragmatic and that pragmatism guided his clear belief in Australia's nationhood and sovereignty.

Menzies demonstrated that when he addressed the issue of the relevance of the Privy Council as the highest court of appeal for Australian law. He said, "I have no doubt, and most lawyers would I think agree, that the High Court of Australia is, and has for been for a long time, composed of a body of judicial lawyers which has no superior in the English-speaking world." Menzies believed in our lawyers, our justice system and believed it had no equal. On this, he is still right.

From that position he questioned appeals to the Judicial Committee of the Privy Council sitting in London. This arose after the Privy Council essentially declined to judicially determine disputes between the powers of the commonwealth and the states or between state and state, as these were considered to be internal squabbles capable of determination by our own judiciary.

Menzies had the vision to take this wider and suggest that the whole system of appeals to the Privy Council needed review. He argued that perhaps we could make the High Court the final arbiter of Australian law and Australian courts. Why should we need to revert to England to interpret and adjudicate our uniquely Australian disputes and laws?

This line of thinking was surprising at a time when Australia was more English than England, a time when the Royal Family was venerated, and when Royal tea cups and commemorative plates were collected by Australian homemakers and stored in cabinets with the 'good' tea service.

Menzies understood that our nationhood evolves, and it still evolves today.

Tony Abbott has often said of Australia that "we have an Indigenous heritage, a British foundation and a multicultural character". His argument is that we may have imported our parliamentary and legal frameworks, but we have made them ours. We have made them uniquely Australian.

Modern Australia might be little more than 200 years old. What we have done is carry with us is almost a millennium of legal history and made it ours. That's why in 1952 when Bob Menzies heard that a small school in the United Kingdom was putting up for sale one of the four surviving copies of the 1297 Magna Carta he snapped it up for the princely sum of £12,500. His opponents argued it was an extravagance, it wasn't. He was forever reminding Australians that eight centuries of hard won rights were no longer just British rights but Australian ones as well.

A country without a free and fair legal system and a contestable parliament, is a system were rights and freedoms depend on the whim of a leader. Our system of parliamentary government has delivered peace, stability and a harmonious diversity that is the envy of the world. True, we are over-governed, but mostly, our Federation works, and our states see themselves as siblings rather than rivals. In a wonderful Australian way, our rivalries are mostly kept to the rugby field.

In a time of Trump, tribalism, social-media partisanship and the new totalitarians who are reigning in China, Russia and elsewhere, it is easy to feel like the world is becoming less moored. That might be true, but Australians should take confidence in our liberal democratic system. In our system 'Jack and Jill are as good as their master', the people have a parliament which gives them a voice and a justice system which treats them equally.

Like every parent, I worry about the world of the future, in which my two beautiful teenage children will grow and give service. I hope they will be lawyers, politicians or take on careers where they serve. I also hope that their lives are spent in the best Western democracy in the world – Australia and that on our watch, and theirs, the principles of our liberal democracy, backed up by our impartial judicial system, will continue to hold strong and true. As it was for Menzies, even in the darkest days of the axis powers, so it must be for them.

31
THE NATURE OF DEMOCRACY

Nicolle Flint

Australians have an interesting relationship with democracy. Unlike most other nations, we did not have to fight for our right to vote.

We did not have to wage war to govern ourselves, or to decide what form our government would take.

Instead, our democracy arrived quietly. Self-government was progressively handed to the Australian colonies in the mid-1800s and has remained intact.

Australian democracy is a bit like a family heirloom; handed down through the generations whether wanted or not.

As with some heirlooms, not all our family members appreciate this precious gift.

Despite the fact our democratic system of government is one the reasons we live such a peaceful and prosperous existence, we know that today, many Australians take it for granted.

Thanks to surveys of current opinions, like that conducted by the Lowy Institute, we know that democracy has never been less valued or valuable to our citizens.

As the Lowy Institute states:

> [O]ne of the most striking findings in our polling history has been about the value Australians place on democracy. Over the last six years, Australians, particularly young

Australians, have consistently indicated a surprising ambivalence about democracy as a system of government.

In fact only 40 to 50 per cent of Australians aged 18-29 believe democracy is preferable to any other kind of government.

It's easy to understand why. Our big, isolated island has been relatively untouched by war and the threat of invasion because we're just too far away for most other nations to think about attacking us.

This also means that although we read, and now see, a lot about the troubles our neighbours and friends have suffered in their quest for independence or to protect their freedoms we haven't personally experienced similar threats.

While we were under threat from the Japanese during World War II, with no Hitler, Mussolini or Stalin to terrorise our citizens or threaten us as neighbours, complacency about our democracy has been the predictable human response.

Our complacency has been encouraged by the additional fact that for decades Australians have enjoyed economic prosperity and growth unrivalled by any other country.

We enjoy a quality and length of life our forebears could scarcely imagine, enjoying historic national, economic and food security. It is not surprising, then, that so many take so much of this for granted. In fact, needing to worry about things like debt and food and national defence seems almost quaint.

Democracy seems pretty quaint, too, because it is largely unchanged from what it was in Menzies' time.

As Menzies' described in his original essay on the nature of democracy, at its most basic definition, democracy is the process whereby each and every man and woman of voting age can exercise their individual choice about who they want to govern our nation.

The Nature of Democracy

The vote of each and every Australian carries equal weight to decide the Members of Parliament. From these Members we draw Cabinet Ministers and the Prime Minister, who together form the Executive and are in charge of governing the nation. Democracy remains government by the people rather than government by a dictator or a despot.

Perhaps because Federation was so recently achieved at the time Menzies was writing, he felt no need to explain the underpinnings of our democracy and the checks and balances inherent in it. These are fundamentally important features that are not discussed nearly often enough these days.

Federation was established to unite the Australian colonies and to provide for a national government to make decisions on limited and carefully chosen issues such as external affairs, national security and defence and trade. Federation was also intended to preserve competition between the states so that the best jurisdictions would flourish and act as a mechanism to encourage less careful or less innovative governments to do better. These finer points have been whittled away by both major parties when in power federally to the extent that our democracy is poorer for it.

Similarly, our continuation of the system of constitutional monarchy expressed through our Westminster Parliamentary tradition has also provided stability, checks and balances on our government and protection of our democracy. These conventions and systems reach back to the Magna Carta in 1215 and have slowly evolved since to the point they have today.

The beauty of our constitutional monarchy is that we are ruled by a Monarch whose powers are largely reserved and unwritten, but can be invoked if there is a constitutional crisis. Reserve powers protect our system of government that has been forged and nuanced over centuries from interfering legislators and litigants.

Also by convention and through our constitution, our federal Parliament is comprised of a government, opposition, a lower house and upper house, our bureaucracy is independent and largely non-party political, and our courts and churches are independent and separate from the state.

We should not, but we always do, underestimate and neglect to promote the importance of our Judeo-Christian values that inform and underpin our constitutional monarchy and thus our Westminster parliamentary tradition and our democracy.

All of these features of our democracy hinge upon each and every citizen exercising their vote and being bound by the rule of law.

Our system, particularly here in Australia, works well. We live in safety. We want for very little. We can afford to care for those most in need.

As in Menzies' time, it is the striking success of our democracy that poses the biggest risk to the system. Achieved after 'centuries of and evolution' as Menzies noted, the 'instrument of popular self-government was then complete'.

Menzies' rightly identified then, as now, that at this point 'democracy's task did not then end; it began'.

With record numbers of Australians ambivalent about democracy, or considering it no better than 'any other kind of government', it is up to our Members of Parliament, our educators and our civic leaders to change this view. We must do more to teach the history of our inherited traditions and to promote the great freedoms and protections they provide to all our citizens. The task of democracy is as important now as it was in 1942; it is a task that must never end. It is a task each of us must assume because as Menzies' wrote 'it is only that democracy which sees the superb spiritual value of the individual man which can really win a crusade against tyranny and force, and lead the way into a better world'.

32
THE SICKNESS OF DEMOCRACY

Trent Zimmerman

There is something wondrous about election days in Australia. When every three or four years, Australians join the queues at schools, church halls and community centres it is perhaps the only time we physically witness that great principle of our liberal democracy: the self-government of equals.

For in those queues – whether it is the thousands at large city polling booths or the handfuls in our smallest country hamlets, we see the distinctions of age, means, experience, background all give way to our belief that each person's judgement is of equal value to that of the next.

It is also the one day of the political cycle when the guns of our political leaders largely fall silent. Weeks and years of campaigning, positioning and proselytising instead falls to the tens of thousands of volunteers who man the polling booths and who, in those few final moments before voters cast their ballot, attempt to secure the support of voters for their Party or cause.

For the candidate, polling day is seen through a fog of exhaustion and the final reserves of adrenalin as the clock ticks towards 6.00 pm when the final votes are cast. As they tour polling booths to thank their volunteers or to persuade the final undecided voter they will encounter the full range of forces that will determine their political fate: from the disinterested to the diehards; from the cynical to those that believe passionately in their individual power to shape their municipality, state or nation.

Few of those candidates will have the time, mental energy or in some cases the inclination, to reflect deeply on what Menzies described as that "moving force" of democracy which they see unfolding on those polling booths. Yet all are players in this incredible phenomenon which, on our own shores and globally, has been the foundation of prosperity and security, the protector and enabler of individual rights and opportunities and the beacon for billions who aspire for freedom and a better life.

For those of us born in nations where the democratic ideal is considered a birthright, these things are easily taken for granted.

The reality of the history of democracy is, however, one marked by struggle and setback as much as it is by fulfilment. With its shoots in the ancient marketplace of Athens (and in some societies, earlier still), its ascendency was slow and tortured. In more modern times, its path was aided by both evolution and revolution, as reason awakened parts of the world – most notably the nations of Europe and north America – to the intrinsic worth and rights of their individual citizens.

The great achievement of the 20th century was the establishment of democracy as the default governing ideal. In a century marked by the readily demonstrable evils of dictatorships, the collapse of colonialism and empires, the shadow of the Cold War and the failings of Soviet and Maoist communism, the case from democracy was one that could be readily made.

How far we have progressed is reflected in the fact that when Menzies spoke of the sickness of democracy in 1942, only a score of nations stood alongside Australia in sharing democratic government.

At the end of the 20th century liberal democratic ideals seemed unstoppably ascendant. Yet the first two decades of this century have, at least dented if not shattered that complacency. The US-based Freedom House, has described 2018 as the year in which democracy faced its most serious crisis in decades. It tracks a slide in democracy and civil liberties commencing in 2006 which has seen 113 countries regress matched by only 62 which have recorded a net improvement.

For political scholars, participants and observers, such trends are difficult to fathom in an era where globally our citizenry has more opportunities than ever before. Across the planet, people are living longer, healthier, with better education, in less poverty and with more opportunities created by the winds of trade, technology and communication. A person today faces less risk from armed conflict or crime than ever before. In short, there has never been a better time to be alive.

Globally there is a sickness in our democratic ideals that eludes easy diagnosis.

In reality there is no single cause.

The end of the Cold War, which shaped many of us born of that era, do not provide the negative reference points that contrasted democracy so favourably. The battle of communism versus democracy is no longer at the heart of global discourse.

As Freedom House reported:

> Perhaps ... most worrisome for the future, young people, who have little memory of the long struggles against fascism and communism, may be losing faith and interest in the democratic project. The very idea of democracy and its promotion has been tarnished among many, contributing to a dangerous apathy.

Our old assumptions that individual liberty and democracy must surely follow economic development and freedom has been undermined by the perceived success of China in offering its people greater prosperity and security despite the repressive and authoritarian nature of its political and civil institutions.

The forces of change that have brought progress and new opportunities for most have also caused disruption for many and resentment towards the political systems that are blamed for upending lives. Technology has empowered the majority but left some feeling ill-equipped in a world where the pace of scientific change is so fast.

Similarly, an area often under-explored are the political consequences of our success in living longer. A century ago average life expectancy was almost three decades shorter for those of us living in nations like Australia. The generational gap between a teenager today and those in their senior years is now so much greater and has served to profoundly accentuate differences between the expectations, lifestyles, values and experience of the young and old. We see this tension manifest itself in debates ranging from same-sex marriage to climate change.

The rise and fear of global terrorism since the World Trade Towers tumbled has, sometimes with justification but often without, created a security premium in government policies, eroding civil liberties previously regarded as sacrosanct within our democracies.

Globalisation, despite its incredible benefits, has undermined a sense of belonging, created forces that are perceived as outside the control of individuals and their governments and fuelled a counter-reaction manifested in increased nationalism.

The inter-connectedness of our economies has, combined with increased American isolationism, discouraged nations from confronting powerful authoritarian regimes and anti-democratic forces. Our economic interdependence has bought our silence on too many occasions.

And equally, a current of cultural sensitivity which, well-meaning and a reaction to the racism and colonialism of past centuries, has produced a timidity in extolling the virtues of the democratic liberal values most associated with what could be typified as western ideals.

The result of these economic and cultural factors is that 20th century democratic evangelism has become mute.

These forces have all combined to erode confidence in many of the representative institutions that have been at the heart of our democracies.

Politicians have often struggled to respond to these challenges. In the broader sense, the rise of new political actors (often on the extremes or under the banner of populist and nationalist policies), have left the established players divided as to whether to accede to what seems to be a different set of values in their communities or to defend and maintain established orthodoxies.

Equally, 'disruptive' technology – be it in the way of communicating with voters or the changing media landscape – have caused a profound shift in the tools of politics. The decline of 'old' media and the rise of new sources of information – particularly through social media – has changed the way in which politicians interact with their voters and many have failed to adapt.

The development of our own Australian democracy has been unique. We became a nation though discourse, at times rancorous, but never violent. We sought to meld the great traditions of Westminster with a federal structure akin to the model our founding fathers observed in the United States. Our democratic ideals were not radical but were, in so many ways, ahead of their times.

Democracies in the 20th century, particularly in Europe, came under enormous pressures – be it the rise of fascism and communism, the worldwide violence of 1968 or the destructive anarchism of anti-globalisation campaigners. Australia has never been immune from these global movements – yet rather than becoming waves that crashed down on democracy's defences, they more gently lapped at our shores.

In a decade of growing cynicism about democracy, Australia has experienced its own disruption and debates about the effectiveness of our parliaments, governments and the major political parties. These have been exacerbated by the apparent failings of some of the institutions previously regarded as the bedrock of our economy or our community. New political players have emerged who have sought to tap into this sentiment and made governing more challenging.

The great moderation of the Australian people has meant that while the voices of those arguing for more radical solutions – both on the left and the right – have become louder and more frequently influencing outcomes at the ballot box, we have not seen the scale of disruption found in other democracies. No major Australian political party has put forward a Trump or a Sanders or a Corbyn as its panacea and the 'sensible centre' of Australian politics would shun such solutions.

It would however be wrong to deny the implications of these forces – to assume that they are transitory, or simply found on the extremes or that don't require us to consider how we can do better – for the disquiet and frustration about the our political processes runs deeply.

In some ways, such cynicism is not new. Menzies argued 75 years ago there is "a good deal of contempt for Parliament, and it has given to the word 'politician' a connotation and flavour – a sort of sneering quality". His own diagnosis of the ills of Australian democracy are heard as strongly today: the quality of those standing for public office; the influence of a media interested in the superficialities of politics; the need for long-range thinking and the call for courage in leadership that was above the ordinary.

Diagnosing a sickness is often much easier than finding the cure and those passionate about our representative democracy are scrambling for treatments. Yet we are seeing the body politic respond in a way which gives cause for optimism.

We see this in the recognition that more needs to be done to restore faith in our democratic institutions – be it in tempering the influence of third parties or foreign players whose interests are not those of the broader Australian community, or in developing those long-range policies Menzies hoped for that go beyond the 24-hour news or the three year political cycles.

However, more fundamentally, the solution lies in showing less timidity and more evangelism in arguing the case for those values at the core of our liberal democracy.

A common theme of Menzies in *The Forgotten People* is the responsibilities, not just the rights, that are afforded in a democratic society.

We have the responsibility to move beyond the glib scripted 'talking points' that have become part and parcel of regimented politics because as parliamentarians we owe honesty and forthrightness to those who elect us.

We have the responsibility to ensure that our representative institutions ensure that the rule of the majority does not exclude those with whom we disagree because fundamentally our democracy is founded on the worth of every individual and their dreams and aspirations.

We must recognise that our evangelism for freedom must not stop at our front door or the borders of our nation. We have the responsibility to uphold our values around the world as their intrinsic might is not dependent on geography, history or culture.

Fundamentally, the principles of our representative democracy are as sound and relevant today as they ever have been.

Our mission must be a liberal nation – not in the partisan sense – but one in which our cherished birthright of freedom and the opportunity to chart our own course in life is at the core of our democracy.

Australia is a relatively new nation, yet we are one of the oldest and most successful continuous democracies in the world. We are not perfect and, at times, democracy has had its ills. But it has proved resilient because, at its core, the values of democratic liberalism are those that have shaped our incredible national journey.

So next time we are in that queue on polling day, distracted by the smells of an election day sausage sizzle or the over-enthusiasm of those handing out how-to-vote cards, we should pause, even just for a moment, to marvel on that moving force that has allowed us to be our own masters.

33
THE ACHIEVEMENTS OF DEMOCRACY

Jonathon Duniam

Democracy is as important today as it has ever been It is the foundation of a stable, free society. As Menzies said: "democracy, being founded upon the rights of the individual citizens, concerns itself first and foremost with the domestic wellbeing of its people."

Because the alternatives to democracy are so grim, we must never take it for granted.

And because the freedoms provided to all men and women are so precious, they must never challenged, reduced or taken away.

Australia is one of only a handful of countries that have enjoyed the stability of democracy continuously since establishment. It is the triumph of Australia.

When Menzies spoke of our democracy in 1942, Australia was fighting for its freedoms against fascism and militarism. We had lost tens of thousands of young men in battle, young men who were fighting to preserve what was good about this country and those it was allied with. It is this hard won freedom that we are at risk of taking for granted today.

In present times while certain parts of our world may be in turmoil we, in Australia, live in an age free of such threats on our doorstep.

However, we must be alert to the temptation to take this for granted. Robert Menzies called on the words of Baron Macaulay in his History of England to highlight how we, when times may be perceived as difficult, long for better ones:

> It is natural that, being dissatisfied with the present, we should form a too favourable estimate of the past.
>
> In truth we are under a deception similar to that which misleads the traveller in the Arabian desert. Beneath the caravan all is dry and bare; but far in advance, and far in the rear, is the semblance of refreshing waters. The pilgrims hasten forward and find nothing but sand where, an hour before, they had seen a lake. They turn their eyes and see a lake where, an hour before, they were toiling through sand. A similar illusion seems to haunt nations through every stage of the long progress from poverty and barbarism to the highest degrees of opulence and civilisation. But, if we resolutely chase the mirage backward, we shall find it recede before us into the regions of fabulous antiquity.

This highlights to readers another mirage being created by the enemies of democracy today. As noted, democracy is concerned with the wellbeing and advancement of the individual and the liberal values that underpin democracy are geared squarely toward that.

At the very beginning of Menzies' Forgotten People speeches we see reference to the desire to divide the nation, a symptom of "the greatest political disease".

In dissecting the recent public comments of a bishop he said:

> He sought to divide the people in Australia into classes. He was obviously suffering from what has for years seemed to me to be our greatest political disease – the disease of thinking that the community is divided into the rich and relatively idle, and the laborious poor, and that every social and political controversy can be resolved into the question: What side are you on?

Today that is as much a reality as it was then, and the contents of the original Achievements of Democracy bear that out. The mirage that Menzies spoke of, sadly, is alive and well.

The political messaging we hear today and the narrative that is employed in contemporary debates by those who seek to undermine true democracy are aimed at encouraging an attitude of reliance on government through terms like 'working poor' and 'working class'. Instilling in the audience that the struggle they have is one that is as a result of society, that it is the government's fault and there is nothing they can do to assist themselves or promote their situation.

This messaging is about creating that division that Menzies spoke of three quarters of a century ago. And while no one, not a soul, would argue that our successful western democracy should not help those in genuine need, the aim here is about creating that dangerous and destructive view that people, themselves, are not responsible for their individual success, but rather that society and government owe it to the individual and the individual owes nothing to society.

At its ugliest, it is about ensuring that people think that anyone who has done well, anyone who has done better than them, anyone who has succeeded or gone ahead has done so at the expense of those who have not. It is about ensuring that people envy and begrudge those who have, as a result of their own initiative, succeeded.

The suggestion that government knows best, that they will ensure that people, no matter how much or how little they try, will all get an equal outcome, is one that is purely dangerous. It is not democracy. It is not fairness, as it is often referred to these days. It is socialism.

Such a suggestion cultivates a destructive attitude of complacency, one of dependency and removes responsibility from the individual for the improvement of their own situation.

This assault on democracy that we currently face is not like the overt one the world faced in 1942, but a more subtle and more measured threat. A threat that is nonetheless just as dangerous.

This threat uses elements of democracy to conceal the fact that it is a danger to our society. The proponents of the arguments against reward for effort and the freedoms and liberties that democracy affords us, are masters of using the English language to try and create the mirage that Menzies spoke about.

For example, terms such as 'fairness', 'equality' and 'big end of town' are often employed to create the perception that a proposal to create competitive taxation conditions for business is one that is geared at ripping off the 'working class'. The perpetuation of such a perception is one that undermines the attitude that Australians can do better for themselves as a result of their own work.

Those who are part of this challenge to democracy, claiming that liberal values and those who support them are not delivering for the individual, are part of the danger to democracy.

It is important to consider the achievements that Menzies pointed to when again reflecting on the words of Baron Macaulay in his writings, *The History of England*, Menzies said:

> Ten or fifteen years have been added to the average life of man. Public health and hygiene have so improved that we take cleanliness and sanitation for granted. Adequate water supply, pure food, clean drains, a sewerage system which has practically destroyed typhoid fever, immeasurably better houses, domestic security backed by an honest and intelligent police, an educational ideal which has given the average man a degree of knowledge undreamt of a century ago ...

These are the fruits of democracy and, pushing our minds back even further in time we see some amazing events in history that highlight democracy as the true shining light for the future of civilisation, including the abolition of slavery.

We can not put too fine a point on it. Democracy creates a world where individuals are left in charge of their destiny and have a say over where they're going in life and how they will get there. This is how we get the best out of people and society.

In summarising what we have in this great country as a result of the achievements of democracy, I consider the stories told to me by my wife and her family, who lived in Albania as part of the final generations to be subjected to the disgraceful form of so-called government, communism.

They tell me stories of deprivation of liberty at concentration camps as a result of dissent. They tell me of being directed by the government where to live, and what vocation they would have. They tell me about the inability of that society to look after its people without adequate resources.

Most telling is how that country failed to advance. Healthcare, education, standards of living all went begging in the time communism reigned in that country. And when compared with Australia and where she is today, it sums up perfectly the achievements of democracy.

It is easy to forget in these modern times, where we have always known democracy and nothing else in Australia, what this institution and those who fought for it have ensured that we modern Australians have in the way of life: freedom, opportunity, good health, good education and all the basics to make a go of things.

We must, as we were as a nation in 1942, remain vigilant to the things that threaten or erode our democratic foundation. Those things that subtly take away our rights, remove our desire to do well and improve our lives for ourselves and our country.

It means reflecting on what we have. We are a nation blessed with natural resources and abundant potential. This requires from us our gratitude and our efforts. By striving to protect our democracy we ensure that those generations that come after us have not just the same, but much, much more.

34
THE TASK OF DEMOCRACY

Peta Seaton

In framing the tasks of democracy, Menzies was thinking about how Australians could reclaim their individual rights and responsibilities after a war-time period in which they had temporarily surrendered certain powers to executive government.

Our modern context has some structural similarities. Islamic-inspired terrorism and the voluntary adoption of consumer technology has regretfully, and in some cases enthusiastically, seen us surrender privacy and autonomy.

And we now see the genius of our philosophical opponents on the left who have refined the art of losing the battle but winning the structural war.

The opponents of true freedom take a long and patient view. Countries may reject communism, socialism and fascism, but the resilient left will quietly infiltrate and appropriate community organisations like an incubus. In Russia, Germany and China they replaced the church with the state, turned neighbourhood boy scouts into troops. In Australia they determinedly colonise the public service, the public broadcaster, public meteorology and science, private workplaces, school committees, and now superannuation corporations and industry groups. Volunteerism (emergency services, local land-care) becomes incrementally institutionalised in their hands. Like the frog in the saucepan, we discover that the organisations that we used to know as grass roots are now effective, funded arms of another ideology, while we at the centre and right have been busy running our businesses to create the wealth that they tax and spend.

So, like Menzies I look to how democracy can provoke a contemporary circuit breaker and with 'mission accomplished' achieve the second of his identified tasks, which is to "restore the authority and prestige of Parliament as the supreme organic expression of self government".

It will only be by the will of the people, and their recognition that their *'consent to be governed'* has been respected, that this prestige will be conferred.

The task of modern Australian democracy is to give back opportunities for choice and self determination to all of us, and in doing so encourage and enable "the good of man" who is "strong, self-reliant, intelligent, independent, sympathetic and generous".

These characteristics are timeless in a culture born of the classical liberal tradition which looks to individuals over government to do what needs must. Australian equivalents of the civilians who jumped onto their fishing boats and sailed to Dunkirk: unpaid Red Cross home nurses, whose descendants are our CWAs who feed the volunteer firies, and the Lions Club members who sizzle sausages at Bunnings to help out a local family. These are Menzies' people – who by day are teachers, truckies, plumbers, and small business people.

Just as we consent to the extent of government we will tolerate, so should we be able to consent to choices to govern ourselves and to individually accept the benefits and consequences of those responsibilities.

Consent is an undervalued element in our policy world.

Whilst we honour consent in many transactions; business arrangements; tenancies; marriage; sexual behaviour; the use of our data; the re-use of our organs; our governments deny people the power to consent out of statutory systems. In fact we are prevented from taking personal responsibility for our own futures in areas such as employment arrangements, childcare, health services, education, how indigenous people might optimise their share of the value in communal land rights, and until recently, same sex marriage. Sometimes the penalty for being self-sufficient can be jail. And tort law has abetted this erosion of democratic choice – by over-riding personal consent in the consequences of personal injury, and by upholding challenges to a person's last will and testament.

Here are some practical ways we could refresh and refocus the task of democracy, reduce costly government duplication and restore personal responsibility to those who want it.

Immediately extract the Commonwealth from domestic health, education, and human services and devolve any Federal powers, and associated dollars, to State or local jurisdictions. We never consented to be governed Federally on these matters. The duplication is a waste of money.

Set term limits for most executive roles in the public sector. The public service has successfully crafted a myth that a full time, fully superannuated, highly regulated role involves a level of sacrifice that ordinary people don't bear. In reality, the majority of today's public service is paid generously whilst enjoying tenure and protections that leave main street employers agog.

The public service includes some of the most fascinating, rewarding, influential roles in Australia. The chance to occupy these roles is a privilege conferred by consent of the people.

Surely it is reasonable that executive jobs in the public service should be shared between a greater number of skilled and experienced Australians over time. If we were to set term limits on these executive roles, we could see more Australians seek to contribute within their own government for a period of their career, and those who incline to public sector roles understand this is not a seat for life.

We must renew our understanding of the true foundations of government. The true public servants are not those well numerated in protected jobs in the Parliamentary triangle, they are, in fact, the nations' small business people who produce the wealth and taxes that pays for the public sector.

Let the supporters of the ABC 'own' it. It's not a constitutional obligation to run a public broadcaster, and any freedom-loving sceptic should be wary of any such institution in a functioning liberal democracy. It tilts the playing field against market and community-supported broadcasters. Claims and counter claims of institutional bias in the ABC are unresolvable. So if we can't all agree, let's offer real choice: those who love their ABC can put their own hard-earned back into a private-subscription ABC – and it can prosper to the extent it is truly supported or earns its keep by sponsorship (so those without means can still access it).

We can then give all Australian taxpayers their share of their involuntary contribution back in a tax rebate. That proverbial '2 cents a day' is now more like fourteen. That's $50 of precious newly-liberated private dollars I would like to use to support the market broadcasters and journalists I choose. I could support free to air by buying more of the stuff they advertise or subscribe to user-pays programs.

Menzies chose a private radio network, 2UE, for his 1942 Forgotten People broadcasts, and they were published by Messrs Robertson and Mullens Ltd of Melbourne at their own cost. Australia has a long history of private support for an accessible media marketplace of political and democratic ideas.

Let consenting award-payee adults decide to make their own private arrangements with employers. It is illegal for a public

The Task of Democracy

sector bus driver or nurse to do a bespoke deal with a boss. This offends the intelligence, rights and responsibilities of consenting individuals in a liberal democracy.

Let consenting adults opt out of statutory childcare and healthcare systems and make their own considered arrangements for themselves and their families, with willing marketplace partners.

In the case of the health system, even if I was to be prepared to keep paying all my Medicare levies and private health insurance obligations, and pay all over again into a market arrangement of my choosing, both I and the brave health services marketeer could be jailed.

We complain about the impossible costs of childcare – which are the result of regulation creep. Yet I am not allowed to contract with an unregulated provider and make my own risk and benefit assessment, and put a value on the fact that I've known the carer for years, and that neither her house nor my house have the Rolls Royce fit-out of the local childcare centre. There may even be peanut butter.

It may be a relief to fainter-hearted politicians that they will have been excused the need to made tough reform decisions, and can at last say 'don't blame me, the person made this choice'.

This would be a welcome step to re-establishing weakening links between individuals and their communities in the civil domain. The anti-freedom movement has cherished the insidious creep of state substitution for what used to be personal decision making and building of trust. I'd rather trust my family, my neighbour or my volunteer colleague to have my back, than a government.

I take heart that digital natives are already making their own work-arounds – their version of opting out of big government. So far the growing gig economy is proof that people are finding their own ways to eschew dinosaur taxi models and traditional hospitality formats. AirBnB operators averaged $7,000 a year income last year, and around 30% of Australians have freelanced in the last year. These personal choices surely evidence an appetite for individual choice and self determination.

And no-one should expect that renewed opportunities for personal consent will be without incident.

These are rights and responsibilities that should never have been taken away. And their gradual erosion saw government monopolies take the place of choice and personal responsibility.

Democracy is messy and involves persuasion, negotiation, and development of compelling ideas. Enabling its important task will require good men and women to be prepared to stand up to those who shoot messengers and ideas.

The task of democracy requires evidence, thoughtfulness, trial and error, and ultimately faith in the overwhelming decency of Australians. By respecting these values, encouraging people to take responsibility to the best of their capability, and strengthening those chords between citizens and the limits of government, we will be best placed to achieve Menzies ambition and restore the authority and prestige of Parliament.

35

THE IMPORTANCE OF CHEERFULNESS

Tim Wilson

A friend has a habit of taking photos of the reflected morning light on Sydney Harbour. Across the waters of Australia's emerald city we see the revealed gold and rose of a refracted dawn. They are shared on social media with #NoOneHasStuffedTheDayUpYet.

That is the wonder of morning. It is a reset. Its embracing fresh glow brings hope, opportunity and optimism for a new day. A fulfilled life comes with this attitude and a perspective to appreciate these moments and their renewing power.

The spirit of successful liberalism is this optimism of a perpetual Australian dawn.

This renewal necessitates appreciating the calming force between people at the beginning of each day brought about through civility. Civility reflects one of the most endearing features of liberalism to thrive: it's faith in people. Civility empowers people to work together in an environment of trust, even without established relationships, to advance the human condition.

Civility recognises that people left to their own devices will take responsibility for themselves, their families and their community; and when supported with the right framework will be entrepreneurial to the benefit of themselves and their community. Civility depends on unspoken boundaries, institutions and the market that formalise legal and commercial engagements and a mutual respect for each other's humanity.

Civility is necessary for order. Cheerfulness is essential for common shared achievement.

Cheerfulness is the attitude to step beyond mere civility. It is the choice beyond mutual respect to see the good in cooperation for individual and community success.

The cheerfulness of a nation informs its choices. The choice Australia has faced has always been the same: do we want to be a social democracy, or a liberal one? Social democracy seeks to anaesthetise people from the realities of life. To assume gloom, and that only collective action can save people from what may be.

Liberal democracy knows that big government delivers small citizens, and that a life exposed to reality is a life full of learning and experience; and that reward can't be achieved without risk and responsibility. Liberalism necessitates a love of life, and everything it has to offer.

Liberals know life is full of struggle. When our opponents see struggle they see the downward pressure that can break a person. They see the pending crush of Atlas under the globe. From physics we learn that every force has an equal and opposite force. We see the Titan's strength and the determination to carry the struggle and their perseverance of their spirit.

The most engaging tool in our political armory is this attitude. There will always be some captured by the idea that today is bad and tomorrow will be worse. Their appeal is rarely what they can do to make tomorrow better. Instead they appeal to a better yesterday.

The politics of fear is an easy temptress. It gives politicians an effective weapon. Too many politicians do not understand it is, at best, a tactic, not a strategy. The pursuit of division ultimately exhausts itself as, just like socialism and money, the dead hand of fear eventually runs out of 'in' and 'out' groups to exclude.

By comparison the politics of hope and aspiration is strategy.

It is sustainable and appeals to our individual and shared ambition for a better world full of freedom, opportunity and justice. It is inclusive because of the potential of individuals, to form families as the foundation for community and in turn, the nation. It appreciates our inheritance and recognises our potential to continue building on the legacy of our forebears. It is an acknowledgment that the book of humanity has been started, and every generation has a worthy chapter within them as do their descendants.

Liberal democrats and social democrats may disagree on the journey of our nation, but we still have more in common than the enemies of democracy. Menzies noted that humour was absent Hitler and Mussolini. It is no more present in Kim Jong-Un or the Mullahs of Iran. Concentrations of power can't tolerate questioning. There is a reason Islamists attack cartoonists. When terrorists attacked Charlie Hebdo they couldn't tolerate mockery of the ideas held dear or see the room for disagreement.

Cheerfulness reflects perspective. It is an understanding that while Parliamentary politics is a serious business, and may be much at stake, it is also a contest of ideas. It is a battle where participants are opponents but not enemies. To see that opposition without malice necessitates requires assuming good intentions.

We can learn from Menzies' legacy. Not only did he rebuff the idea that politicians from differing sides could not be friends, he built lasting relationships with those that he furiously disagreed. After the deaths of both John Curtin and Ben Chifley, men he had opposed in general elections, Menzies served as a pallbearer at their funerals. Menzies saw their common humanity and their patriotism before their disagreements.

The modern obsession by the progressive-left to curtail what can be debated, what can be discussed and the language we can use sharpens the ever-seriousness of our polity. Humour can be hate. Ridicule is rejected. Verbiage may be violence.

A "windy side of care" isn't just a mindset, it is an anchor that politics is about people's relationships to each other, and society. That attitude is particularly important in Australia. We have always been a people facing the common enemy of an untamed island continent, more than each other. That is our bond.

Our politics was not founded on grandiose ideals, or stemmed from conflict. There was no revolution. British academic Hugh Collins describes Australia's unique political culture as of "schemes for representation, legislation, and administration [as] a detailed exposition of the institutional means of securing that public good which maximizes private interest". We are utilitarian and not wedded to classical ideals. There is a reason we use the term "ideological" disparagingly; it is the political equivalent of a wowser - someone who is so wedded to their own ideas that there isn't room for the lived human experience.

Our culture evolved from the necessary larrikinism to survive the plight facing newly arrived convicts and free settlers in a harsh terrain to build a modern nation. Laconic and acerbic wit has become necessary for Indigenous Australians in facing the consequences of European settlement. And we share a mutual appreciation for self-deprecation because anyone who takes themselves too seriously shouldn't be in charge of anything. They are ingredients of a national character that allies itself with Sir Les Patterson and the Foxy Ladies of Fountain Lakes on a Bran Nue Dae.

If you want to make a point: say it. If you want to make it memorable: joke it.

Reflecting on contemporary politics, American economist Russ Roberts has argued that "the underlying problem is very old. Most of us know little. The world is a complex place and it's hard to know what is going on. So we grope around in the dark trying to make sense of what is happening and what explains what we observe".

This is becoming increasingly difficult in an age of social media.

Many people often remark that social media has given a platform to turpitude. That's right. The only thing that has changed is the platform. The people and their arguments always existed. They were just absent a publisher.

What is changing is contact. Words without human expression beget bluntness. The human face always gives context. Technology can remove it.

Twitter is harsh because it is often anonymous. And also because it is often just words leading even anodyne comments to escalation. By embracing anonymity, people present as online drones unconscious and distant from the destruction they wreck.

It is why Facebook is more moderate because words accompany pictures through invited friendships. It is why facial emojis soften all communication and no one ever gets into an argument on Instagram.

The need for light-heartedness, warmth and humour as vehicles for human connection is amplified considerably for politicians on the centre-right. One of the great risks facing responsible centre-right politicians is to think and communicate in ideas and systems. By its nature these arguments are depersonalised and detached.

Comparatively, centre-left politicians are normally dripping with empathy and speak through human stories.

The problem that faces our opponents is that their arguments sustain themselves in isolation, but can't when taking them society-wide. They've learned the worst traits of companies seeking a subsidy: find a willing victim, abuse them as a prop to communicate their empathy with disregard to the interests of all others and whether it can be afforded consistently. It's only when the absurdity of their position is exposed that they're defeated – but it must be done without malice or disinterest to the human experience.

As Bert Kelly demonstrated with devastating effect in his Modest

Member columns, there were many good intellectual arguments that protectionism could survive; but bad ideas cannot withstand ridicule. We must be happy warriors for our cause and engage with warmth and charity, and through the lived condition. Ours should be infused with optimism that allows us to talk about ideas in a way that generates connection and hope.

Ultimately, cheerfulness is an essential precursor for successful public service. The uniting purpose of public service is a love of community and country, coupled with an appreciation of the opportunity to deliver improvements for people. Cheerful public service embraces the opportunity to pursue liberalism as a just cause for humanity and that embraces every new day with a constant victories attitude.

The Contributors

The Hon Tony Abbott MP is the Member for Warringah and the 28th Prime Minister of Australia. He was Prime Minister from 2013 - 2015 and is the fourth longest serving leader of the Party serving from December 2009 until September 2015.

Between 1996 and 2007, Tony Abbott was successively parliamentary secretary, minister, cabinet minister and Leader of the House of Representatives in the Howard government.

He has been Member for Warringah in the Australian Parliament since 1994.

Tony Abbott has degrees in economics and law from Sydney University and an MA in politics and philosophy from Oxford which he attended as a Rhodes Scholar. He is married to Margaret and they are the parents of three adult daughters.

Louise Ahern has served as speechwriter to a Prime Minister and two State Governors.

She worked as a Ministerial Adviser in the Howard Government. As Superannuation Adviser to two Assistant Treasurers she was proudly involved in the abolition of end benefits tax on superannuation and the simplification of regulation. As an adviser to the Honourable Dr David Kemp AC during his tenure as Minister for Environment and Heritage, she worked on the introduction of Australia's first national heritage protection system.

With a law degree and an arts degree majoring in government, Louise is the third generation of her family to be involved in conservative politics. She is raising her two sons, Ben and Thomas, to be proud Queenslanders.

Adam Boyton has over twenty years experience across economics, public policy, politics and financial markets. He has been the Australian Chief Economist for a global investment bank as well as the Chief of Staff to a NSW Opposition Leader. He started his career in the Australian Treasury and the Department of the Prime Minister and Cabinet.

Adam is a regular contributor to the policy debate and writes for the *Australian Financial Review*. In 2016, he was named by Deloitte and Boss magazine as one of 50 outstanding LGBTI business role models.

Adam is a member of the Paddington Branch in Sydney's eastern suburbs.

Andrew Bragg is the author of the short book, *Fit for Service*, and formerly worked as an accountant, think tanker, financial services executive and Acting Federal Director of the Liberal Party. He regularly writes for national and NSW newspapers – his articles are filed at andrewbragg.com

Andrew joined the Party in his home town of Shepparton, Victoria in 2001. He is currently President of the Paddington, NSW Branch.

Michaelia Cash is the federal Minister for Jobs and Innovation. She was elected as Senator for Western Australia in 2007.

Senator Cash's previous ministerial appointments include Assistant Minister for Immigration and Border Protection, Minister Assisting the Prime Minister for Women, Minister for Employment, Minister for Women and Minister Assisting the Prime Minister for the Public Service.

She joined the Liberal Party of WA in 1987 and is a member of the Moore Division.

Nick Cater is the Executive Director of the Menzies Research Centre, a public policy think-tank affiliated to the Liberal Party of Australia.

He is a former journalist and senior editor at the Australian. He began his career at the BBC in London and has worked for News Limited in Adelaide, Canberra and Sydney, and as a foreign correspondent in Asia.

Nick is the author of *The Lucky Culture: And the Rise of an Australian Ruling Class* (2013) published by Harper Collins Australia.

Peta Credlin is a strategist and policy professional with over sixteen years' experience at the highest levels of Australian politics. Peta Credlin was Chief of Staff to the Prime Minister, the Hon Tony Abbott MP, between 2013 and 2015. First joining his office when he was elected Leader of the Opposition in 2009, Credlin served six years as his chief of staff and ran the leader's campaign in the 2010 and 2013 federal elections. She joined the Howard Government in 1997 and previous roles as a ministerial adviser included the portfolios of defence, communications, immigration and foreign affairs.

Now a SKY NEWS anchor and political contributor, Peta Credlin also writes a weekly column syndicated nationally.

Born and raised in country Victoria before finishing her secondary education in Geelong, Peta has a Bachelor of Laws from the University of Melbourne and a postgraduate in law from the Australian National University (ANU). She has been a member of the Liberal Party of Australia (Victorian Division) for almost 20 years as a member at large and served on the executive of the Victorian Liberal Women's Council.

Georgina Downer is an Adjunct Fellow at the Institute of Public Affairs. Georgina has extensive experience in foreign policy, both inside and outside government. She has worked at the University of Melbourne as the Director of Asialink Diplomacy, and was previously a diplomat at the Australian Embassy in Tokyo.

Georgina has worked as a corporate lawyer at Minter Ellison Lawyers in Melbourne, and as a researcher for US Senator Chuck Hagel and the Baroness Howe of Idlicote in the House of Lords, UK. She is director of the Indigenous arts project, The Torch.

Georgina was awarded a National Scholarship to study Commerce and Law at the University of Melbourne, and a UK Foreign and Commonwealth Office Chevening Scholarship to undertake a Masters in Public International Law at the London School of Economics.

Georgina is a member of the Warrandyte branch and has been a member of the Victorian Liberal Party for four years.

Jonathon Duniam is a sixth generation Tasmanian, currently serving as a Liberal Senator for Tasmania. Born in North-West Tasmania, currently residing in Hobart, Jonathon was elected at the 2016 double-dissolution election.

Prior to the election, Jonathon has been professionally involved in politics for some time, including as serving as Deputy Chief of Staff to the Tasmanian Premier, Will Hodgman. Jonathon has been an active member of the Liberal Party in Tasmania since 2001, commencing as a member of the Young Liberals and then various branch and electorate executive roles in the southern Tasmanian electorate of Franklin continuously ever since.

Jonathon believes that the Liberal Party is the best party to realise the potential of Australia's future, embracing the philosophies that bring out the best in people.

Senator the Hon Concetta Fierravanti-Wells is the Minister for International Development and the Pacific. Prior to this, she was the Assistant Minister for Multicultural Affairs, with responsibilities in the Attorney-General, Immigration and Border Protection, and Social Services portfolios.

She also served as the Parliamentary Secretary to the Minister for Social Services, with special responsibility for multicultural affairs and settlement services and has been a Senator for New South Wales since 2005.

Senator Fierravanti-Wells has had a long association with the Italo-Australian community and in 1995 was made a Knight of the Order of Merit of the Italian Republic.

She holds a Bachelor of Arts in Political Science and European Languages, and a Bachelor of Laws.

Having joined the Liberal Party in 1993, Senator Fierravanti-Wells has been a member of various branches including the NSW Italian Special Branch and the Newport Branch

Paul Fletcher is the federal Minister for Urban Infrastructure and Cities and Member for Bradfield.

Before entering Parliament in 2009, Paul was a senior executive at telecommunications company Optus; and earlier in his career Chief of Staff to the Minister for Communications in the Howard Government, Senator Richard Alston. He has dual first class honours degrees in law and economics from Sydney University and an MBA from Columbia University in New York where he was a Fulbright Scholar.

Paul joined the Liberal Party in 1981 while at high school, and today is a member of the Lindfield Branch.

Nicolle Flint MP was elected as the federal Member for Boothby in 2016. She is the first woman to hold the seat since it was established in 1903. Nicolle serves on the House of Representatives Standing Committee on Tax and Revenue, the Joint Committee of Public Accounts and Audits and the Standing Committee on Communications and the Arts.

Nicolle attended Flinders University in Boothby and graduated with a double degree in Law and Arts.

Nicolle has represented small and medium businesses at the Australian Chamber of Commerce and Industry in Canberra, provided policy advice to Liberal leaders Dr Brendan Nelson and Malcolm Turnbull, and more recently has worked as a columnist for The Advertiser and The Age newspapers. She is the co-author of the Menzies Research Centre Paper Gender and Politics which examines the representation of women in the Liberal Party.

She is a member of the Waite Branch and has held senior leadership roles in the Liberal Party of Australia (SA Division) including on State Executive.

Ross Fox joined the Liberal Party in his first year at the University of NSW. He has held leadership positions in both the NSW and Victorian Liberal Divisions. Ross was the Liberal candidate for Isaacs in south-east Melbourne at the 2007 election. From 2008 to 2013 he was elected to the Administrative Committee in Victoria and held the position of Vice-President from 2011 to 2013. Ross ceased his involvement in partisan politics on becoming the Executive Director of the National Catholic Education Commission in July 2013.

Ross is the Director of Catholic Education in the Archdiocese of Canberra and Goulburn, a position he has held since December 2016. As Director he leads a system of 56 Catholic schools with more than 21,000 students across both the ACT and southern NSW.

Ross holds honours degrees in Engineering from the University of NSW and Philosophy, Politics and Economics from the University of Oxford. He has worked as a business consultant, policy advisor to state and federal politicians and as an educational administrator. He is currently a Director of the Australian Council for Education Leaders.

Josh Frydenberg was elected in 2010 as the Member for Kooyong.

He has been Minister for the Environment and Energy since July 2016, having previously served as Minister for Resources, Energy and Northern Australia, Assistant Treasurer and Parliamentary Secretary to the Prime Minister.

Josh has Law and Economics degrees with Honours from Monash University and completed his articles of clerkship at Mallesons Stephen Jacques. He also has a Masters in International Relations from Oxford University and in Public Administration from the Harvard Kennedy School of Government.

He was Senior Adviser to Foreign Minister Alexander Downer and Prime Minister John Howard and a Director of Global Banking at Deutsche Bank AG.

Josh Frydenberg joined the Liberal Party two decades ago and is a member of Balwyn Branch.

Cam Hawker is a PhD candidate at UNSW Canberra at ADFA where he is completing research on Australian Prime Ministers and the ANZUS alliance. He has also worked at UNSW Canberra an Associate Lecturer.

Prior to this, Cam was a Canberra based adviser for the Liberal Party, both in Opposition and then in Government. Cam worked in a variety of roles on defence and foreign policy. He is a Presidential Associate of the Australian Institute of International Affairs (AIIA) and a member of the Australian chapter of the Council for Security Cooperation in the Asia-Pacific (Aus-CSCAP)

Cam has been a member of Victorian Division of the Liberal Party since 2009.

Senator Jane Hume is a Liberal Party Senator from Victoria, having been elected in July 2016.

Born and raised in Melbourne, Jane Hume completed a Bachelor of Commerce at the University of Melbourne and later returned to gain further qualifications in Political Science.

Senator Hume has held various senior positions in the financial services industry, working for the National Australia Bank, Rothschild Australia, Deutsche Bank and, immediately prior to her election, as a Senior Policy Advisor at Australian Super. She has also served on a number of boards including the Royal Children's Hospital, Federation Square, and Perinatal Anxiety & Depression Australia.

Following her election in 2016, Senator Hume was immediately appointed as Chair of the Senate Standing Committee on Economics (Legislation).

Jane Hume joined the Armadale Branch of the Victorian Division in 2003. Her passion for female participation in politics saw her awarded the 2013 Couchman Scholarship by the Liberal Women's Council, where she developed a formal mentoring programme aimed at equipping the next generation of female political leaders.

Julian Leeser MP has been the Federal Member for Berowra since 2016. He is co-chair of the Joint Select Committee on the Constitutional Recognition of Aboriginal and Torres Strait Islander Peoples.

Prior to his election to Parliament he was a lawyer, company director and senior executive at Australian Catholic University. He spent nearly seven years as a custodian of the legacy of Sir Robert Menzies as Executive Director of the Menzies Research Centre.

He joined the Liberal Party in 1992 and is a member of the Westleigh Fox Valley Branch.

Senator Jim Molan AO DSC was declared an elected Senator for NSW by the High Court of Australia in December 2017. He was a Liberal candidate for the Senate in the 2016 election.

Prior to entering the Senate, Jim had served in the Australian Army for forty years. He retired in 2008 as a Major General.

Jim served as a field commander, infantryman, a helicopter pilot and a military diplomat in Papua New Guinea, Indonesia, East Timor, Malaysia, Germany, the US and Iraq. For "distinguished command and leadership in action in Iraq", Jim was awarded the Distinguished Service Cross by the Australian Government and the Legion of Merit by the US Government.

In August 2008, Jim published his best selling book *Running the War in Iraq*. Following the 2013 election, Jim was appointed the Prime Minister's Special Envoy for Operation Sovereign Borders (the border control operation). Jim recently participated in an international ethical evaluation of Operation Protective Edge (Israel's military action in Gaza 2014) and an investigation of the threat to Israel of Lebanese Hezbollah.

Jim is a member of the Queanbeyan branch of the Liberal Party and has been a leader of the Democratic Reform Movement of the NSW Liberal Party.

The Hon Kelly O'Dwyer MP was elected to Parliament in 2009 as the Member for Higgins. She is currently the Minister for Revenue and Financial Services, and in December, 2017 she was given additional responsibilities as the Minister for Women and Minister Assisting the Prime Minister for the Public Service. She has previously served as the Minister for Small Business and Assistant Treasurer.

Kelly is a member of Cabinet's Expenditure Review Committee. She is the first woman in a Federal Cabinet to hold an economic portfolio, and in 2017 became the first serving Cabinet Minister to have a baby. Kelly has been a member of the Liberal Party's Victorian Division since she was 17.

Senator James Paterson is a Liberal Senator for Victoria. Elected to fill a casual vacancy in March 2016 at age 28, he is the youngest ever Liberal to serve in the Australian Senate.

He is Chair of the Senate Finance and Public Administration Legislation Committee and Deputy Chair of the Modest Members Society.

Before he joined the Senate, James worked at the free market think tank the Institute of Public Affairs for five years, finishing as its Deputy Executive Director.

James joined the Liberal Party at age 17 in Caulfield, where he remains a branch member today.

The Hon Dr Peter Phelps MLC is a member of the NSW Legislative Council. He joined the NSW Liberal Party in 1984, aged 16, and is currently a member of the Queanbeyan Branch.

Christopher Pyne joined the Liberal Party in 1984 and is a member of the Burnside branch of the South Australian Liberal Party. He was elected to the House of Representatives for the seat of Sturt in 1993.

He is the Minister for Defence Industry, and Leader of the House of Representatives, responsible for delivering the $200 billion build up of Australia's military capability, the largest in our peacetime history.

Christopher has been a Minister in the Howard, Abbott and Turnbull Governments serving as Minister for Ageing; Minister for Education and Training; and Minister for Industry Innovation and Science.

Christopher is the author of *A Letter to my Children*, published in 2015. Before entering Parliament, Christopher practised as a solicitor. He is married to Carolyn and is the father of Eleanor, Barnaby, Felix and Aurelia.

Christopher Rath joined the NSW Young Liberals in 2006 at just 16 years of age. He has been the President of the Throsby Young Liberal Branch, based in Wollongong, for over ten years.

Christopher has a decade of political and professional experience in roles ranging from a policy adviser in the Baird Government to a public affairs manager in the mining industry. He is currently the Government Relations Manager at IAG, Australia's largest general insurance company.

He was elected to the NSW Liberal State Executive in 2015. Christopher's interest in economics and the battle of ideas started in high school and continued at the University of Sydney where he formed the Conservative Club while completing a Bachelor of Economics and a Master of Management.

Senator Linda Reynolds CSC was sworn into the Senate in July 2014 as a senator for Western Australia.

Prior to entering the parliament, Senator Reynolds has over 20 years experience at the national political level working for Ministers, Members of Parliament and the Liberal Party of Australia. Her appointments include being Chief of Staff to the Minister for Justice and Customs and Deputy Federal Director of the Liberal Party.

Senator Reynolds has almost three decades of experience as an Army Reserve Officer, serving in a range of part and full-time appointments. She was the first woman in the Australian Army Reserves to be promoted to the rank of Brigadier.

Her defence appointments include being Commanding Officer of a Combat Service Support Battalion and Adjutant General of Army, the Chief of Army's key governance advisor. She was awarded the Conspicuous Service Cross in 2011.

Senator Reynolds joined the Liberal Party in 1987 and is a member of the Burt Division in WA.

Paul Ritchie is the Senior Writer for Speech-Write a consultancy providing communications support for business, political and community leaders. Paul has worked for four state and federal party leaders. He was Head of Communications and Senior Adviser to Tony Abbott during the Abbott Prime Ministership.

In 2009, Paul received his Master in Public Administration from the John F Kennedy School of Government at Harvard University. As well, Paul holds a Master of Business Administration (Executive) from the Australian Graduate School of Management and a Bachelor of Business from the University of Technology, Sydney. Paul is the author of two books: *Stay on Message* published by Vivid in 2010 and *Faith, Love and Australia. The Conservative Case for Same-Sex Marriage* published by Connor Court in 2016.

Paul Ritchie joined the Liberal Party in 1983 and is a member of Seaforth Branch.

Senator the Hon Scott Ryan is the President of the Senate and a Senator for Victoria.

Scott joined the Essendon West branch of the Liberal Party in 1990, and is now a member of the Melbourne branch. He served as Chairman of the Party's Constitutional Committee, as a member of the Administrative Committee and as Metropolitan Vice President before being preselected for the Senate at the 2007 election. He was also a key member of the Futures Committee that enacted extensive party reforms in Victoria, in particular plebiscite preselections and much wider ballots for party elections.

Scott was re-elected in 2013 and 2016 and has served as a Parliamentary Secretary for Education, Assistant Cabinet Secretary, Minister for Vocational Education & Skills, Special Minister of State and Minister Assisting the Prime Minister for Cabinet. He resigned from the ministry on 13 November 2017 to become 25th President of the Senate.

Scott is married and lives in Melbourne with his wife and two sons.

The Contributors

Dr Peta Seaton AM is a leader in public policy and strategy. As a former NSW parliamentarian and front-bencher representing the Southern Highlands she served as Shadow Treasurer amongst several other portfolios, and served as Director of Transition, and Strategic Priorities for Premier Barry O'Farrell.

Peta consults to private and public sector CEOs, and is Chair of Australian Hearing, Director (Assoc) of BDCU Alliance Bank, Director Menzies Research Centre, and the Near Eastern Archaeology Foundation. Peta joined the Liberal Party in 1995, inspired by her experiences as a shop assistant, small business owner, TV and advertising producer, and her work with NSW Premier Nick Greiner.

Andrew Shearer is senior adviser on Asia-Pacific Security at the Washington-based Center for Strategic & International Studies (CSIS), one of the world's leading national security think tanks. He is also director of the CSIS project on alliances and American leadership and C.D. Kemp Fellow at the Institute of Public Affairs.

Andrew Shearer was previously national security adviser to Prime Ministers John Howard and Tony Abbott. In that capacity, he played a leading role in formulating and implementing Australian foreign, defence, and counter-terrorism policies. He has more than 25 years of experience in intelligence, national security, diplomacy, and alliance management.

Andrew Shearer was director of studies at the Lowy Institute for International Policy, and his analysis has been published in books, journals, and leading U.S., Australian, and Asian newspapers. He holds a master's degree in international relations from the University of Cambridge and honours degrees in law and arts from the University of Melbourne. He was awarded a UK Foreign Office Chevening Scholarship.

Dean Smith was selected as a Liberal Party Senator for Western

Australia in May 2012. He is currently the Government Deputy Whip in the Senate.

In 2014 he was an early advocate for reforms to Australia's free speech laws and an original co-signatory to a Private Senators Bill to reform Section 18C of the Racial Discrimination Act 1975, and in 2017 he was the architect and author of a successful Private Senators Bill that legislated for equality before the law for same sex relationships in Australia.

In February 2018 was named the inaugural winner of the McKinnon Prize for Political Leader of the Year.

Prior to entering Parliament, Dean had held executive positions with two of Australia's most prominent companies, Insurance Australia Group (IAG) and SingTel Optus.

Dean has been an active member of the WA Liberal Party for over 30 years. He is currently a member of the Inglewood Branch and Associate Member of the Albany and Port Hedland Branches.

The Hon Tony Smith MP is Speaker of the Australian House of Representatives. He has served as the member for the Victorian electorate of Casey since the general election of 2001.

He was the Parliamentary Secretary to the Prime Minister, the Hon John Howard in 2007. He has served on numerous parliamentary committees throughout his career, including as chair of both the Joint Standing Committee on Public Accounts and Audit and the Joint Standing Committee on Electoral Matters.

He was elected Speaker in August 2015 and re-elected in August 2016. He is the thirtieth Speaker since Federation.

Before entering Parliament, Mr Smith was senior political adviser to the then Treasurer, the Hon Peter Costello. He joined the Liberal Party in 1988 and was president of the Melbourne University Liberal Club the same year.

The Contributors

The Hon Alan Tudge MP is the Minister for Citizenship and Multicultural Affairs and Federal Member for Aston. He was elected to Parliament in 2010, appointed Parliamentary Secretary to the Prime Minister in 2013, and was Minister for Human Services in 2016-2017.

Prior to entering Parliament, Alan had a broad career including several years with Boston Consulting Group in Australia and New York, Senior Adviser to Ministers Alexander Downer and Brendan Nelson and Deputy Director at Noel Pearson's Cape York Institute.

He has degrees in Law and Arts from Melbourne University, and an MBA from Harvard. He is married with three children. Alan joined the Liberal Party in 2004.

The Hon Malcolm Turnbull MP is the Prime Minister of Australia and the Member for Wentworth. He was first elected as the Member for Wentworth in 2004.

Since entering parliament, Mr Turnbull has held a number of parliamentary including Parliamentary Secretary to the Prime Minister with responsibility for national water policy, Minister for Environment and Water Resources, and Minister for Communications.

He was Leader of the Opposition from 16 September 2008 to 1 December 2009.

He became Prime Minister of Australia on 15 September 2015.

Malcolm was educated at Vaucluse Public School and Sydney Grammar School and graduated from Sydney University with a BA LLB. He was awarded a Rhodes Scholarship and completed a further law degree at Oxford.

Malcolm first joined the Liberal Party in 1973 and is a member of Point Piper Branch.

The Hon Natalie Ward MLC was elected to the Legislative Council of the NSW Parliament on 21 November 2017. She currently serves on a number of Legislative Council Standing and Select Committees.

Natalie is the Duty MLC for the Northern Province and is a member of Manly Business Branch.

Prior to her election, Natalie was a lawyer, practising in commercial litigation and financial services, both in federal regulatory practice and in the private sector.

Natalie also serves as a Director of the Australian Rugby Foundation Board (now Rugby Australia). She is married to David Begg and they are busy raising two teenage children (her most vocal constituents).

Tim Wilson is the Federal Liberal Member for Goldstein and formerly served as Australia's Human Rights Commissioner and a policy director at the Institute of Public Affairs.

He has a Bachelor of Arts and a Masters of Diplomacy and Trade from Monash University, and a Graduate Certificate in Energy and Carbon Management from Murdoch University.

He first joined the Victorian Division of the Liberal Party at age 18 and is a member of the Beaumaris Branch.

Ken Wyatt AM MP is a proud Noongar, Yamatji and Wongi man and was elected in 2010 as the Federal Member for Hasluck, the first Aboriginal Member of the House of Representatives.

In 2015, Ken became the inaugural First Nations member of the Federal Executive after being sworn in as Assistant Minister for Health, and in January 2017, he again made history as the first Aboriginal Minister to serve in a Federal Government, after being appointed Minister for Aged Care and Minister for Indigenous Health.

Before entering politics, he worked in the fields of health and education including as District Director for the Swan Education District, and Director of Aboriginal Health in New South Wales and Western Australia.

In 1996, Ken was awarded the Order of Australia in the Queen's Birthday Honours list. Later, in 2000, Ken was awarded a Centenary of Federation Medal for 'his efforts and contribution to improving the quality of life for Aboriginal and Torres Strait Islander people and mainstream Australian society in education and health'.

Trent Zimmerman MP is the federal Member for North Sydney.

He is a former State President of the NSW Liberal Party and served as a Councillor on North Sydney Council for eight years. Prior to entering Parliament in 2015, Trent was Deputy CEO of a major tourism and transport industry association.

Trent joined the Liberal Party in the 1980s and is a member of the North Sydney Branch.

The Forgotten People: Updated

www.ingramcontent.com/pod-product-compliance
Lightning Source LLC
Chambersburg PA
CBHW052105230426
43671CB00011B/1937